ITS LIGHT IS THE LAMB

AN UNEXPECTED SPIRITUAL JOURNEY

Edna Mc Grew

by EDNA MC GREW

ISBN 0-7414-4242-6

Published by:

INFINITY
PUBLISHING.COM

1094 New DeHaven Street, Suite 100
West Conshohocken, PA 19428-2713
Info@buybooksontheweb.com
www.buybooksontheweb.com
Toll-free (877) BUY BOOK
Local Phone (610) 941-9999
Fax (610) 941-9959

Printed in the United States of America

Printed on Recycled Paper

Published October 2007

This book is dedicated to
my beloved husband, David,
without whose encouragement and support
Its Light Is the Lamb
would never have been completed.

"I saw no temple in the city;
for its temple was the sovereign Lord God and the Lamb;
and the city had no need of sun or moon to shine upon it;
for the glory of God gave it light,
and its light is the Lamb."
(Rev. 21:22-23)

PREFACE

When I was 18, I entered Mt. St. Mary's Abbey in Wrentham, Massachusetts. It had just opened as the first Cistercian (Trappist) abbey for women in the United States. Surprisingly, I knew nothing about mystical contemplation when I entered. I simply felt that it was God's will that I become a Cistercian nun. However, when I left more than two years later because of an erroneous x-ray diagnosis, I not only knew something about contemplation, but, from that point on for the rest of my adult life, I felt a call to contemplative prayer.

This book is the story of my contemplative journey, which was revitalized after I took early retirement. It is also a testimonial to four people who helped me on this spiritual journey. These include: Sister Nancy Mullen, who resides in Long Island, New York, USA; Dr. Gianna Talone-Sullivan of Emmitsburg, Maryland, USA; Mrs. Vassula Ryden, the Greek Orthodox mystic who presently resides in the USA; and lastly, Father Thomas Keating, mystic, author, former Cistercian Abbot, and founder of Contemplative Outreach, presently residing in St. Benedict's Monastery, Snowmass, Colorado, USA.

TABLE OF CONTENTS

INTRODUCTION

When I was a preteen during World War II, I kept hearing everyone say, "We were fighting a war to end all wars!" I was young and optimistic. I believed that our civilization was rapidly advancing to a point where wars would be limited and occur mostly in third world countries. However, a few years after World War II ended, America was again fighting a war, the Korean war. This was followed by the Vietnam War and the Gulf War! And in the background, as it were, the Cold War lurked, ever threatening to engulf the world in a catastrophe of unprecedented proportions.

It seems as if I have lived my life in the shadow of continuous wars. Yet we here in America have never really felt the impact of these wars in any way comparable to how each of us must have felt when the two airliners crashed into the Twin Towers of the World Trade Center on September 11, 2001! Now, as I think about all this, I am appalled by this mystery of evil which seems to overhang our world. And yet I still believe in God, a God of goodness. It is this God that I want to write about; particularly, this tender and loving Father whom I have come to know in the years since I took early retirement.

ONE

THOSE PRE-RETIREMENT YEARS

A short time after I was born, I was baptized into the Roman Catholic faith. I don't ever remember religion or God being discussed at home during my early childhood. Yet it must have been, in some form or another, because I can remember once going to Sunday Mass with my father when I was about five years old. I wondered how everyone in the church that Sunday morning could be still and quiet for so long a time. I came away with the impression that spending time praying to God was a very difficult thing to do.

After I finished the first grade in public school, my parents moved to a new neighborhood. My mother enrolled me in the nearby catholic elementary school sponsored by the Holy Child Jesus Church in Richmond Hill, New York. It was in that church that I made my First Communion. While I can remember my white dress and my white shoes, I cannot remember receiving the Eucharist! What stands out most in my memory of that day was how bad I felt when all the girls, except me, received a bouquet of flowers upon exiting the church. Those are the only memories I have of my First Holy Communion!

As you can see from the above example, God was not important in my life at that time. However, when I reached the age of about nine or ten, things suddenly changed. I can clearly remember receiving communion at a First Friday Mass celebration which the whole school attended every month. After returning from the altar, I knelt down in the pew and, all at once, I found my heart overflowing with love for God. This happened every time thereafter, whenever I received communion. I do not remember it happening during the rest of Mass or any other time of the day or week.

This experience continued for a number of years, although it was no longer as strong as it had been in the beginning. Now, as I look back, I realize that those experiences were special gifts from God. The power of these experiences – that they were more than just an emotional reaction to receiving Communion – is evidenced by their fruits. That is, by the fact that, shortly after this first occurred, I started going to daily Mass and sometime later, I started to say the Rosary every day.

After completing grade school, I continued my education in Queen of All Saints and Bishop McDonnell High Schools in Brooklyn, New York. When I graduated from high school, I already knew that I wanted to become a Trappist Nun. It so happened that a group of Irish Cistercian (Trappist) women were planning at that time to start the first foundation of their order in Wrentham, Massachusetts at the request of the Bishop of the Archdiocese of Boston. In order to be accepted by the order, in addition to the appropriate letters of recommendation as to my character and suitability as a candidate, I was required to provide a dowry of $1,000 plus an additional sum of money each month until I took my vows. So I went to work for a year in an insurance company in midtown Manhattan to earn that dowry. My sister, Pat, agreed to pay the additional monies that were required monthly.

I entered the Monastery on September 8, 1950. My mother was heartbroken but she never said a word to discourage me. I was the second daughter my mother had given to the Lord, as one of my older sisters had already entered a missionary congregation. I remained with the Trappist nuns for a little over two years. Except for the first two weeks, those were two of the happiest years of my life. I did not want to leave. But I was having a problem with my neck and the doctor ordered X-rays taken. Mother Superior told me that these X-rays showed that my "first cervical was ankylose and that there was a partial ankylosis of the second cervical." She told me that the doctor had informed her that I would only get worse. She pointed out that under the Trappist rules, since I had not yet taken final vows, that I would have to leave. She gave me a note to give to the doctor when I returned home. I still have that note.

When I got home and went to see the doctor and had a second set of X-rays taken there was no evidence of any problem whatsoever. However, at this point, it was obvious to me that my mother needed me at home. I ultimately decided that God was using the circumstances of my life to make clear to me that my vocation to be a Trappist had been a valid, but temporary vocation, and that it was no longer His will that I be a Trappist nun. But that left me with the question: "What did God want of me?" or "How could I serve Him now?"

After a couple months of rest at home, I took a course in Speedwriting, and got a job as a legal secretary with a firm in downtown Manhattan. Subsequently, I enrolled in the City College of New York. It took me five years to get my Bachelor of Science degree cum laude with a major in Physics. During four of those five years, I attended classes at the uptown campus; worked afternoons, five hours a day at the law firm in downtown Manhattan and spent three hours a day riding a triangular route on the New York City subway system between uptown and downtown Manhattan and my home in Richmond Hill. Riding the subways gave me an opportunity to do my homework. At home, it was necessary for me to share the household chores with my Mom because she worked by the day cleaning the homes of others.

After finishing college, I got a job as Assistant Engineer at the Sperry Corp., a defense contractor, located in Lake Success, NY. While working there by the day, I attended the

Polytechnic Institute of Brooklyn at night and received a Master of Science degree in Electrical Engineering with a major in Computer Science. During my years at Sperry I specialized in computer design. In addition, I pioneered the design of digital signal processors. I became the first women in the company to become an Engineering Research Section Head. I married an engineering co-worker at Sperry. Prior to my husband's retirement, he was the System Engineering Manager for the design and development of the NEXRAD weather radar system which is currently deployed throughout the United States for use by the National Weather Service, the FAA and the Air Force. In 1988, after working 28 years, I took early retirement from the Unisys Corp. (Formerly Sperry)

TWO

THE UNEXPECTED

One afternoon, shortly after I retired, I was exercising on my indoor bike and watching TV. The talk show host was doing an interview with a nun, whom I now think was Sister Briege McKenna, OSC. To my surprise they were talking about apparitions of Mary, the Mother of Jesus. These apparitions, together with numerous signs and healings, were allegedly occurring in Medjugorje, located in Bosnia-Hercegovina. During one of the early apparitions, when asked by the visionaries who she was, Mary identified herself as the Queen of Peace. I had never heard such an interview on TV before and so I listened closely. However, when the TV show was over, I thought no more about the apparitions, probably because of the ingrained suspicion that I had for such stories and the hoopla that are often made over them. And because I didn't usually find I could relate much to what the Catholic Church refers to as "private revelations."

My eighth grade teacher was Sister Nancy Mullen, a Sister of St. Joseph. I developed a friendship with her and usually went to visit her once or twice a year. She had taught grade school for a number of years, went to Puerto Rico to teach there, and then returned to Long Island to teach high school Math. When she was in her fifties, she shared with me that she was looking for something "*more*." She found it in the Charismatic movement. After much prayer and discernment she decided to open a Charismatic house of prayer.

On Aug. 25, 1976, Sister Nancy and five other Sisters of St. Joseph founded the St. Pius X House of Prayer in the former convent of the Sisters of Mercy, Plainview, Long Island, NY. On Feb. 21, 1980, a covenant community of people who desired to be led by the Holy Spirit was established in connection with the House of Prayer. The community consisted of Jesuit priests, Maryknoll Sisters, Sisters of Mercy and Sisters of St. Joseph as well as members of the laity. In April 1984 they formulated their covenant and took the name New Bethlehem Covenant Community. The Community grew from 18 original members to approximately 58 adults and their children. In 1991 the Pius X House of Prayer was moved to the Van Bourgondin House in West Babylon, NY. It remained open until 2003.

On February 6, 1989, I went to visit Sister Nancy in the St. Pius X House of Prayer. She told me that the House of Prayer had a new ministry which was to lead pilgrimages to Medjugorje. She proceeded to tell me about the alleged apparitions of Mary in Medjugorje. She showed me a video. When I left, she gave me a book to read relating to the apparitions. I was very skeptical that there was anything to these apparitions, but because of the respect and high regard in which I held Sister Nancy, I decided to read the book she had given me.

It was a small book, titled *Medjugorje,* published by the Riehle Foundation, containing 12 homilies given by the Franciscan priests of Medjugorje, together with 12 more articles/homilies of various priests from North America. What particularly interested me was the emphasis on prayer. In one of Father Slavko Barbaric's homilies he refers to a "school of prayer" conducted by Mary with "step by step direction."[1] In a homily by Father Jozo Zovoko, he quotes Our Lady as saying: "Don't pray with your lips; when you pray, pray with your heart." Father Jozo confessed that he had difficulty in understanding what the Blessed Virgin Mary meant until she explained:

> *"Today before prayer,*
> *may every one of you forgive your neighbor.*
> *"Today may everyone find in his heart all of his enemies,*
> *and may he show them to the Father with Joy.*
> *"May he pray for them.*
> *"Let him wish full joy and blessing upon them."* [2]

Father Jozo goes on to explain how he told the assembled congregation these words from Our Lady to the visionaries; and then asked all the people in the Church if they understood, and if they could do what Our Lady had asked. There was an uneasy silence and finally Fr. Jozo said:

> "'We will try now to pray for conversion, for the gift of forgiveness.'
> "There was silence for about 20 minutes. It was terribly long. We didn't know where to go.
> "**Then the greatest miracle in Medjugorje that I know of, happened.** The church was crowded with people, and one man in the middle of the church shouted with a powerful voice: 'Jesus, I have forgiven!' And he went on, crying bitterly.
> "Suddenly, that's what every one of us did. Can you imagine, thousands of people crying, and praying, 'Jesus, I have forgiven, forgive me!'"[3] (emphasis mine)

THREE

THE DARK NIGHT

An entry in my journal dated March 7, 1989 reads as follows: "I feel that Medjugorje is a message to me." Recently, as I reread this entry, I was totally surprised! I had no memory of thinking or writing these words! But I do remember the difficulty I had with prayer at that time.

Officially, I had taken early retirement on March 31, 1988. However, since I had accrued quite a number of vacation days which I took during the first three months of 1988, I considered myself retired as of the beginning of that year. The first thing that I started to do in January 1988, was to set aside part of each day for spiritual activities, including attending daily Mass and meditating. I had long planned to do this when I evaluated the possibility of my retiring in my fifties. However, when that time came and it looked as if I could financially afford to retire early, I was scared, very scared.

Because of my fear of retiring I had tried to prepare myself. Three years earlier I decided to test myself. If I could lose weight just by exercising and keep it off, then I felt that I would have a good chance of being able to handle the trauma which retirement would mean for someone like me who had such an A-type personality.

And if I could discipline myself that way, surely I would be able to resume my prayer life which had been drastically reduced when I started attending college and began working as a legal secretary to support myself. After I finished college and started working as an engineer, there still was little time available to me, as I went to school at night for my Master's degree in EE. Since my undergraduate major was not EE but Physics, I had to do a year of make-up work, which took longer than a year in evening school. As I advanced in my career the work became more demanding and I had to work longer hours. Because of my heavy schedules all during those years, I could see no way of resuming my pursuit of mystical contemplation. Sadly, as I look back now, I realize that if only I had known someone to guide me, things could have been very different. My life, at that time, was not incompatible with a life of contemplative prayer in the world, but I didn't know that then!

I began my exercise plan by walking ten minutes a day. I gradually increased the time until I was walking an hour a day, five days a week. When it rained, I would use my indoor cycle and/or rowing machine for an hour. What started as self discipline, became a relaxing and satisfying experience which gave me some confidence in my ability to handle retirement. However, when I did in fact retire, and when I tried to resume a set schedule of prayer, I found that it was extremely difficult for me to do so.

As I knelt each day in meditation, I was besieged with negative thoughts. "Is this wordless form of meditation really prayer? This is such a waste of time; you should be out helping the poor and the needy." I looked for someone with whom I could discuss contemplative prayer. But found no one who seemed interested in this type of prayer. The big problem that I faced was due, I believe, to the fact that, as Father Keating so aptly puts it in his classic book, *Open Mind, Open Heart:*

> "Contemplation was identified with extraordinary phenomena, and was regarded as both miraculous and dangerous, to be admired from a safe distance by the average layperson, priest or religious.

> "The final nail hammered into the coffin of the traditional teaching was that it would be arrogant to aspire to contemplative prayer. Novices and seminarians were thus presented with a highly truncated view of the spiritual life, one that did not accord with scripture, tradition and the normal experience of growth in prayer."[1]

Since I did not read and benefit from Father Keating's book until a number of years later, I continued to struggle with my prayer life. In the years after I left the Trappists, the works of Thomas Merton of *Seven Storey Mountain* fame, were my one big source of encouragement relative to contemplative prayer. It was obvious in his writings that his life revolved around a continuous search for God. Somehow, reading his books always soothed that yearning in my soul that made me feel like a stranger in this world. I read and collected the majority of his works. Two of my favorites included: *Conjectures of a Guilty Bystander* and *Zen and the Birds of Appetite*. But the one thing that I did not find much of in his works was encouragement for the laity in pursuing the path of contemplative prayer. Not that he completely ignored the issue, but just that he seemed to be more concerned about contemplation as it related to the life of the monk and the hermit. Therefore his writings were not much help to me now that I was retired and needed some practical advice and help.

As time went on, even my attendance at daily Mass became a time of trial and interior conflict and I felt isolated and alone. My doubts as to the value of my wordless form of meditation became even more of a burden as I suddenly found that God no longer existed for me! It was not that God was absent; it was, instead, that God simply did not exist. This went on for a long time. I continued to pray but I felt like a hypocrite. Finally I decided that I must just continue to take that "leap of faith" over and over again whenever I prayed.

I reread the proofs for the existence of God and regularly reviewed in my mind the positive thoughts which I had used in the past to convince myself that God did exist. But, to no avail. However, the idea of wasting my life was something I could never accept. Life had to have some meaning, some goal. Otherwise, it was not worth living.

Finally, I decided that I would continuc to seek after and pursue goodness, which had always seemed so beautiful to me, particularly, when I would see someone perform some selfless act of service or kindness to another human being. I determined that I would attempt to show love to my neighbor as best I could. But I knew only too well that trying to live up to my ideals was not that easy. In the past, only prayer had given me strength. So I determined to continue with my prayer life. If God, in fact, did not exist, so be it! At least I would have tried to do something with my life that had more meaning than just living for myself.

Is it any wonder that I felt that Medjugorje was speaking to me? Here I was questioning the value of prayer and what happens? Our Lady starts appearing in Medjugorje, not only stressing the importance of prayer, but teaching us how to pray!

As I indicated above, I had also begun to question the value of my attendance at daily Mass. You can imagine how consoling it was to me to read in one of Father Slavko Barbarics homilies that the Madonna had said: "Let Holy Mass be your life."[2] Later I came across these additional quotations from Mary: "The Mass is the greatest prayer of God. ***You will never be able to understand it's greatness***."[3](emphasis mine) And again she reiterates: "Mass represents the highest form of prayer."[4]

After I finished reading the small book on Medjugorje that Sister Nancy had given me, I decided to see what other information was available. So I went to a religious book store in a nearby shopping mall. I found a book titled

Messages and Teachings of Mary at Medjugorje written by Father Rene Laurentin, who obviously believed in the apparitions. Then I found another book titled *Spark from Heaven*, written by Mary Craig who was an interviewer both on British TV as well as on BBC radio. Glancing at her introduction I felt that she might present a more critical view of these happenings and I wanted to get as diverse a picture as possible. So I bought her book as well.

Now, as I reread portions of her book I am impressed by the thorough job she did in researching her project, as evidenced not only in the written text, but also in her extensive and varied bibliography. In her Introduction, Mary Craig points out that the so-called Balkan Peninsula and in particular, the former Yugoslavia, had a violent history. She quotes a passage from Rebecca West's classic on the former Yugoslavia, *Black Lamb, Grey Falcon* as follows: "Were I to go down to the marketplace, armed with the powers of witchcraft, and take a peasant by the shoulders, and whisper to him, *'In your lifetime have you known peace?'* wait for his answer, shake his shoulders, and transform him into his father, and ask him the same question, and transform him in his turn into his father, I would never hear the word 'Yes', if I carried my questioning of the dead back for a thousand years."[5] (italics mine)

Yet, it is in this place of conflict and suffering, caused by power hungry politicians, ethnic hatreds, the refusal to forgive, and ongoing religious strife, that the Virgin Mary has come, identifying herself as the "Queen of Peace;" speaking of the need for reconciliation; and indicating that:

"The world is on the point of receiving great favors from me and from my Son."[6]

FOUR

MEDJUGORJE

In America we have opinions on every conceivable subject, or so it seems. And we don't hesitate to express them with every confidence in our right to say what we think. Daily we are asked for our opinions on myriads of subjects by TV talk show hosts. But I wonder what answer they would get if they questioned Americans about Medjugorje. It seems very likely to me that many people, if asked, might not have an opinion because they had never heard about Medjugorje, even though the apparitions and messages continue to this day. For this reason I would like to give a brief history of the apparitions.

The drama begins on the afternoon of June 24, 1981. Two teenage girls, Ivanka and Mirjana, go off on a walk in the hills surrounding the hamlet of Bijakovici at Medjugorje in order to relax and have a smoke in secret. On their way back, Ivanka is startled as she suddenly sees the Madonna in the distance. Mirjana refuses to look in the direction her friend is pointing. The two girls run home, fearful of what Ivanka had seen. Later the same day they return with their friend, Vicka, and again behold the Madonna beckoning them to come closer. That evening the girls become the butt of jokes and Vicka's sister teases her, intimating that she had probably seen a flying saucer.

At dusk on the following day, the three girls plus a few of their friends, as well as a small number of people from the village, go to the same spot at the foot of Cronica hill. Our Lady appears at the top of the hill and the teenagers go running and scrambling across the rocks and up to the hill to the spot where she is again appearing. This time six young people, later referred to as the visionaries, see the Madonna.

The next evening, as it was getting dark, the village and surrounding area are "lit up by three flashes of brilliant light."[1] Seeing the light, the youngsters rush up the hill followed by several thousand onlookers, some of whom are carrying tape recorders. Suddenly, close to an old wooden cross, the six youngsters spin around in unison and drop to their knees. Mirjana talks to the Lady who has appeared before them and asks her who she is. In response, the Madonna says "I am the Most Blessed Virgin Mary."[2] Several tapes were made by some of the onlookers. Their existence was reported in a *Sunday Times* article: "Tapes made on the day vividly record the tumult as the children described to the crowd what the Madonna looked like and valiantly tried to transmit questions to her and report her replies."[3]

After this third apparition, as the crowd disperses, Marija feels drawn to go off by herself. Suddenly, she sees:

> "a vision of a cross, shining with a whole spectrum of colors, but empty. In front of the cross, weeping, stood the Madonna. 'Peace, peace, you must seek peace. There must be peace on earth, you must be reconciled with God and with each other. Peace, peace, peace.'"[4]

FIVE

THE MYSTERY OF EVIL

In reading the Old Testament, certain passages seem to indicate that it was the Lord God who hardened the heart of the Pharaoh so that he would not let Moses and his people leave Egypt. However, most biblical passages refer to people hardening their own hearts. I have puzzled over this many times. And as I do I sometimes wonder "What is the nature of evil?" I don't know what the theologians/philosophers have to say about this, but it seems to me that it is surely an unresolved question. And perhaps more so in our modern culture, where intellectuals go so far as to deny the very existence of evil, let alone the existence of Satan!

Shortly after the attack on the Twin Towers of the World Trade Center of 9/11, there was a short essay in Newsweek magazine in which a student at Yale University indicated that she decided to drop a course because of what happened in one of her classes on the day after the Sept. 11 destruction of the two World Trade Center towers in New York City. Her professor said that "he did not see much difference between Hamas suicide bombers (who he pointed out, saw themselves as "martyrs") and American soldiers who died fighting in World War II."[1] She points out that her fellow students appeared to be "uncomfortable assessing, or even asking whether a moral wrong had taken place."[1] Instead they came up with numerous reasons justifying the actions of the terrorists. She goes on to say "The explanation students and professors give for the Sept. 11 attacks – extreme poverty in the Middle East, America's foreign policy in that region and religious motivation – are insightful, but they cannot provide absolution for wrongdoing."[1] She further implies that this kind of ambiguous attitude relative to evil actions in themselves, was the general attitude on campus, not just the view of one professor and one classroom of students.

In a Phi Kappa Phi Forum magazine, which was devoted to the subject of terrorism, Professor Paul Trout discusses the attitude and teachings of American college professors. He claims that: "For forty years, many 'progressive' academics have vilified and defamed the United States [as well as Western civilization]."[2] As I studied up on the history of the Balkans, I got some understanding of why the people of these territories have good reason to criticize some of the political policies of the great powers. But the impression I get from these and other articles is that Americans might be surprised and concerned if they were to sit in on many of the classes in our universities. And they might, indeed, concur with Paul Trout who stresses that "If ideas have consequences, there is no way to avoid the possibility that anti-American hate speech could have helped prepare the way for mass murder."[2]

And in another article in Newsweek, George F. Will identifies "the toxic idea at the core of all the most murderous ideologies of the modern age. The idea is that human nature is, if not a fiction, at least so watery and flimsy that it poses no serious impediment to evil political entities determined to treat people as malleable clay to be molded into creatures at once submissive and violent."[3] This may seem somewhat far fetched to us Americans, but then he goes on to cite an example, which occurred recently in the Middle East, of "A mother rejoicing that her teenage child has blown herself up in the process of blowing up other mothers' children."[3] Or going back to the Nazi atrocities, he indicates that one supervisor of massacres took photographs of Jews as they were executed so that he could entertain his family and friends with the photographs. He summarizes the position of civilization's enemies thus: "These enemies believe that human beings have no common nature, no shared moral sense that is a component of a universal human nature. Rather, all we have in common is a capacity to acquire an infinite variety of cultures, however vile."[3]

As I read about Medjugorje I found myself wondering why did the Blessed Mother seem so concerned and why had she selected this particular place. Was she trying to warn the people of Bosnia-Hercegovina of the need to convert before even greater disasters should befall their country? Or was Our Lady speaking to a larger audience? Why did she make such a cry for peace among individuals, peoples and nations?

In her book, *Spark from Heaven*, Mary Craig points out that this part of the world "has been not only a meeting point between many civilizations, cultures and faiths, but also a scene of their violent collision. It marked the historic divide between East and West."[4] In her second chapter she provides a seventeen-page history of the former Yugoslavia from its historical beginnings until the time Our Lady's apparitions began in the early 1980's. She indicates that Medjugorje is situated in the Brotnjo plateau in Hercegovina in the former Yugoslavia. This area was initially settled by the Illyrians and by the first century AD it was part of the Roman Empire. In AD 395 a frontier is established between the Greek-speaking (Byzantine) and the Latin-speaking Western Roman empires, based respectively in Constantinople and Rome. This border was to play an important part in the history of the Christian Church. Disputes between the pope of Rome and the patriarch of Constantinople, coupled with differences that existed for centuries between the eastern and western parts of the empire, resulted in a schism in AD 1054. It would be more than 900 years before this mutual excommunication was lifted; but the separation created at that time between the two churches remains to this day.

In the sixth and seventh centuries, the area was overrun by Slavonic tribes: the Slovens settled to the north, the Croats to the center and west, and the Serbs to the east of the frontier established in AD 395. In the late 1300's the Ottoman Turks began an invasion of the Balkan Peninsula. Decades of fighting ensued. The Turks ultimately took control of Serbia, then Bosnia and finally, in 1483 Hercegovina fell to the Turks. The Muslim rule lasted for over 400 years.

In 1878 the Congress of Berlin authorized the occupation of Bosnia-Hercegovina by Austro-Hungary. In 1914 the Archduke Franz Ferdinand is assassinated in Sarajevo by a young Serb from Bosnia. As a result, Austro-Hungary declares war on Serbia and the assassination of the Archduke is perceived by world historians to be the precipitating cause of the first World War. In 1918, the Kingdom of Serbs, Croats and Slovens is created with Alexander as its head. And in 1929, Alexander established a royal dictatorship, renaming the country Yugoslavia, land of the Southern Slavs.

In the meantime, Mussolini develops designs on the Balkans. As part of his plans he sponsors terrorist training camps. One of these groups included the Croat nationalists, known as the Ustase. This group had been formed by the lawyer, Ante Pavelic, who fled to Italy from Yugoslavia after Alexander formed his dictatorship in 1929. Mussolini encourages the Ustase to make hit-and-run guerilla raids into Yugoslavia. However, it is not until 1941 that Mussolini's designs are accomplished. In that year Yugoslavia is hit by German bombers who leave 17,000 dead and force an unconditional surrender. Hitler and Mussolini proceed to subdivide Yugoslavia. Pavelic and his Ustase were put in charge of the Independent State of Croatia, which included Bosnia-Hercegovina.

According to Mary Craig "Pavelic wanted to 'purify' Croatia from its alien Serbs – whom he hated – and as a sop to Hitler, from its Jews…Croatia was to be a two-religion state – Catholic and Muslim – again….There began a barbarous persecution of the Orthodox Churches."[5] Many villages of Orthodox Serbs residing in Croatia, were obliterated when one third of the Serb population was killed. As part of his systematic attack on the Serbs, another third of the Serbs was deported and the final/last third, mostly peasants, were forced to convert to Roman Catholicism. In addition, it is estimated that more than half of the 40,000 Jews who lived in the newly Independent State of Croatia were killed.[6] In retrospect, it is easy to believe that these atrocities laid the ground work for the even greater ethnic violence which occurred in the subsequent wars instigated by Slobodan Milosevic.

When World War II ended, Yugoslavia became the first Soviet satellite under Marshal Tito. It was recreated as a Federal Peoples' Republic consisting of six republics: Croatia, Macedonia, Montenegro, Bosnia-Hercegovina, Slovenia and Serbia and two autonomous provinces of Serbia – Kosovo and Vojvodina. Tito's rule of approximately 35 years ended with his death in 1980. With his passing the world press "predicted the imminent demise of Yugoslavia and even a civil war between its constitutent nations."[7]

Shortly thereafter, Our Lady makes her first appearance in Medjugorje. At the same time Slobodan Milosevic was in the process of taking away Kosovo's autonomy as part of his territorial ambitions. But at that time I did not even know who the man was. Nor did I know much about the Balkans or about Bosnia-Hercegovina. When I ultimately read Mary Craig's book, it certainly seemed quite reasonable to believe that if, in fact, Mary really was appearing in Medjugorje and talking so much about the need for peace, she probably intended her messages as a warning for the people who lived in that area.

However, I thought no more about it until the civil wars, predicted ten years prematurely, actually broke out in the 1990's. As soon as I started learning from the TV and in the newspapers of the conflicts in the former Yugoslavia, I began following the news from the area more carefully. I wondered if Sister Nancy Mullen and the other sisters in the House of Prayer were still leading pilgrimages to Medjugorje. It was only much later that I learned that, when the fighting first broke out in Bosnia-Hercegovina, the pilgrimages to Medjugorje ceased. However, in the early part of 1992 Our Lady made it known to the visionaries that she wanted the pilgrimages to be resumed and she said that she would protect them from harm.

When the apparitions first started on June 24, 1981, Father Jozo Zovoko, a Franciscan priest and a member of the Charismatic movement, had been pastor of St. James church in Medjugorje since November 1980. Consequently he had not yet met all of his parishioners, and he says that he did not personally know the visionaries at the time of the apparitions. When he heard about the alleged apparitions, he concluded that they were, in reality, part of a plot to bring discredit on the church. Because of his suspicions about the young visionaries, Father Jozo recorded all of his interviews with them. Apparently, the Communist authorities also thought it was some sort of plot, but in their case they thought it was created by the Croat clergy. As time went on, Father Jozo came to believe that the visionaries were indeed seeing Our Lady, the Mother of God. His continued support of the visionaries antagonized the authorities, who had been harassing the visionaries and who had attempted to close down the church of St. James in Medjugorje. After continued conflict, the authorities sent two agents from the Mostar Ministry of the Interior to arrest Father Jozo. He was subsequently tried and sent to jail for three and some half years. The authorities claimed that Father Jozo was an extremist who intended to restore the terrorist Ustasa organization.

In March 1992, Father Jozo who, by that time was no longer in prison, came to the United States. During his visit, he conducted services at St. Benedict church in Long Island, NY. He told the congregation that the eleventh anniversary of Our Lady's appearance in Medjugorje would occur that June. He encouraged them to come to Medjugorje in June and pray for peace. He told them that Our Lady had indicated that all who traveled on pilgrimage to Medjugorje would be protected from harm by her son, Jesus. The House of Prayer responded to Father Jozo's call and led one of the first groups to resume pilgrimages to Medjugorje. The group was nervous, but set out in faith.

Sister Nancy did not go with that first group which was led by another Sister from the House of Prayer. However, she led subsequent pilgrimages. She remembers one particular pilgrimage which took place shortly after the government had issued some sort of warning to visitors; this had made her particularly nervous. Nonetheless, she went. She relates how she felt one evening when she was walking alone, back from St. James Church, through the village of Medjugorje, to her lodgings. Earlier in the day, she had taken a different path to the church, so she had not seen this part of the village. All of the homes and buildings that she passed on her return were protected against gunfire by sand bags piled high in front of them. She was scared, being all by herself. Over the mountains she could hear the sound of gunfire and mortar. She remembers the relief that she felt when she got safely back to her lodgings. Sister Nancy tells me that during the ten years of civil war Medjugorje remained completely intact, and that Medjugorje was never hit by a bomb although they fell all around the outskirts of the village.

I tried to follow the war and wondered who or what had caused it. However, the stories that I heard were very confusing. I didn't know who was fighting who, nor did I know which causes were just. Consequently, when I began this book I decided that in order for me to see things in perspective, that I ought to do some reading about the almost ten years of civil war in that country during the 1990's, particularly since, during eight of those years, the pilgrimages to Medjugorje continued despite the danger.

In the course of my readings about the demise of the former Yugoslavia, I came upon three theories that have been seriously proposed as to the cause of all these wars. The first is the idea, as Misha Glenny expresses it, that there is "a solid body of Western popular opinion that regarded and still regards the Balkans as a toxin threatening the health of Europe. The chemistry of the toxin is assumed to be too complex for any known antidote."[8] I found the same idea expressed in an editorial in the Charleston Gazette, titled the "Balkan trap, Kosovo hate incurable."[9] After discussing NATO and President Clinton's options in the Kosovo conflict the editorial ends with these words: "we doubt that any resolution will alter the age-old Balkan hates that resurface endlessly in different forms."[9]

Another theory, particularly with regard to the civil wars and wars of succession in the 1990's, is the idea that they were caused by evil leaders such as Slobodan Milosevic, Radovan Karadzic and Franjo Tudjman. In his book *Origins of a Catastrophe*, Warren Zimmermann who was United States Ambassador to Yugoslavia from 1989 to 1992 writes "This is a story with villains – villains guilty of destroying the multi-ethnic state of Yugoslavia, of provoking three wars, and of throwing some twenty million people into a distress unknown since the Second World War.... Yugoslavia's death and the violence that followed resulted from the conscious actions of nationalist leaders who coopted, intimidated, circumvented, or eliminated opposition to their demagogic designs. Yugoslavia was destroyed from the top down."[10]

The third theory does not refer as much to the basic cause of these wars as it does to the idea that the so called "Great Powers" substantially influenced the course of history in Yugoslavia, often quite negatively. Misha Glenny gives a brief history of these interventions. He writes: "Before 1999, the great powers had intervened three times in the Balkans. The first was at the Congress of Berlin in 1878…The second began with the Austro-Hungarian ultimatum to Serbia in the summer of 1914…The third started with Italy's unprovoked attack on Greece in March 1940…These three interventions were so destructive that they guaranteed the Balkans' relative economic backwardness, compared to the rest of Europe. And the violence that these interventions encouraged, often inflicted by one Balkan people on another, ensured the continuation of profound civil and nationalist strife."[11]

While all these theories have merit, I wonder if perhaps we are overlooking something more basic. Has not our modern culture so brainwashed us that we tend to reject the idea of evil? And of personal responsibility? Have we unwittingly allowed Satan to ingratiate himself into our lives? In George Will's article referenced at the beginning of this chapter, he quotes these words of Adolph Eichmann regarding the atrocities perpetrated in Germany during Hilter's time: "Little by little we were taught all these things. We grew into them."[3]

Have we, perhaps, been learning little by little to deny the existence of evil in our own hearts? In a message in 1998 to Gianna Talone-Sullivan Our Lady said: "Do not look at the current affairs of the world and ask 'why has God allowed this?' Look at the current affairs in the world and ask yourself 'why have I allowed this by not responding to God's gift of love?'"[12]

SIX

APPARITIONS IN SCOTTSDALE, AZ

Does God have a special plan for our era? If He does, what is it? It is only recently that I have begun to believe that God may, indeed, have such a plan and that numerous references to it can be found in the Holy Bible. I came to this belief slowly, over a period of more than ten years.

It all started when I went again to visit my friend, Sister Nancy Mullen in the early 1990's. She was the nun who had told me about the apparitions at Medjugorje. Almost as soon as I got there, she started telling me about new apparitions of Our Lady which were allegedly occurring in Scottsdale, AZ. By this time I had come to believe that Mary was probably appearing in Medjugorje. But as Sister Nancy proceeded to tell me about what was happening in Scottsdale I said to myself "No, not another one! This is too much." It didn't fit the pattern that I had in my mind of where Our Lady would appear and, furthermore, I didn't think it likely that, if she were appearing in Medjugorje, that she would also come to the United States!

Sister Nancy spent almost the entire time of our visit talking about the apparitions in Scottsdale. I was a little put out by this. I had come to visit with her and here we were spending almost all of our time together talking about something that I didn't really believe. Something in which I had little interest. When I left, she gave me an audio tape that had been made in Scottsdale. At home I listened to the tape. I just didn't believe it. And as I wrote earlier, I had difficulty relating to what the Catholic Church referred to as "private revelations." And yet something within me prevented me from completely closing my mind to the possibility. I reacted just as I had with Medjugorje, in that I said to myself that, if this were really from God, then I would certainly hear about it again. I had absolutely no intention of curiously pursuing every alleged apparition that was reported.

Some time later a woman in our parish signed up for our Little Rock Bible Study program. She called me to talk about the schedule for the classes. During the course of our discussion she started telling me about the alleged apparitions in Scottsdale. My first impulse was to cut her off, telling her that I had already heard about them. But instead, I decided to say nothing, and just hear her out. She talked for about half an hour. When she finished, I was no more convinced than when she had started. But this was the second time I had heard about Scottsdale. When she offered to lend me a copy of the first volume of the *I am your JESUS of MERCY* books from Scottsdale, I decided to read it.

The first time that I read the book, it was with a certain amount of curiosity, and being a speed reader, I read it fast. As I did, I kept looking to see if anything in it appeared to disagree with or depart from the teachings of the Catholic Church. While some things I read puzzled me, I really couldn't find anything that I thought was contrary to Catholic doctrine. When I finished, knowing that curiosity had been my main motive in reading the book, I asked myself "Suppose this really is from God?" So I decided to read it again a second time, but slower.

As I commenced the second reading, it was like it was a completely different book! My heart was filled with love for, and gratitude to God. I read a few pages a day. Everything I read touched my heart. When I finished reading the book, it was not enough for me, I had to reread it again! And so I read it a third time, slowly and prayerfully, underlining the passages that had special meaning for me. Then I went out and bought the second volume and also read that one slowly and prayerfully, at least three times. Ultimately, I read all six volumes, each at least three times.

What was it about these books that so impressed me? The first volume of the *I am your JESUS of MERCY* books was divided into two parts. The first part consisted of 'Lessons from Our Lord.' In the very first Lesson on the Sorrowful Mysteries of the rosary, Jesus says, not 'do as I do' or 'imitate Me,' but rather **"BE ME!"**[1] To me, this meant only one thing, that Our Lord was calling us to contemplative prayer. That is the only way that I know of in this world to *be Jesus*. Later, Jesus again emphasizes that He wishes us to be Him when, in a very profound but simple statement, He says: "Unity with My Body allows the power of My gifts…love, faith and hope…to be Me, living them in you!"[2]

Part II of Volume 1 contains messages from Our Lord and Our Lady given through the St. Maria Goretti parish prayer groups. Again, just as in Part I, in the very first message from Our Lady she says: "My children, open your hearts to Jesus."[3] In the second message Mary says: "Please place Jesus at the center of your lives."[4] As I read these messages, I kept thinking of Father Thomas Keating's book, *Open Mind, Open Heart*. These messages were stressing the very subject that Father Keating addressed in his classic book on Centering Prayer and contemplation. Not only is Our Lady talking in general of praying with our hearts, but she was making it quite clear that she is referring to contemplation when she refers to: "the people who will not go beyond the prayer of speaking words, instead of the prayer which should be from their heart."[5]

After I finished reading the complete set of Lessons from Our Lord, I was impressed with their progression. They begin with the basic truths of the Christian life explained in clear and forceful language. Yet each Lesson is permeated with words of love and concern for our well being and spiritual growth. As the Lessons continue, they become longer and provide more detailed instructions on the spiritual journey and the fruits of spiritual maturity. To study these Lessons and how they reflect Holy Scripture seem to me to be a very sure way to proceed on the contemplative journey to oneness with God.

The *I am your JESUS of MERCY* books were such a help to me that they became one of my major sources of spiritual direction. They strongly reassured me that God was calling all of us to mystical contemplation. In addition, there were two specific items relative to my spiritual journey that were a very big source of help and consolation to me. I don't remember now where these passages are in the Lessons from Jesus, but I remember the words. One was "Go at My pace;" and the second was "That may not be asked of you."

One of the interesting things that distinguished these apparitions from those at Medjugorje was the fact that not only was Mary appearing to the visionaries in Scottsdale, but Jesus was also appearing to some of them. It seemed to me if Jesus was appearing to some of the visionaries, it must be for a very serious reason. Because of this and because of the very strong impression these Lessons made on me, I decided to go to Scottsdale, AZ. My sister and I made a pilgrimage to Scottsdale in September of 1992. When I went, I had a special spiritual concern in my heart. We spent a number of days there and attended Our Lady's Thursday night prayer meeting. It was September 10, 1992. On that night Our Lord spoke through Fr. Jack Spaulding. It was a very special experience for my sister, who is a nun. I was a little uncomfortable at the idea that Fr. Jack had been used, as he has said, like a microphone! But I did not doubt that it had happened. I just hadn't yet come to an acceptance of God's doing things His way!

After the service, as we were walking across the parking lot, we saw Mary Cook, one of the visionaries, on her way to her car. I approached Mary and told her that I was praying for her. Mary Cook took my arm and gave me such a look of gratitude that I have never forgotten that moment. She looked so beautiful. And as I looked at her, I remembered what our Lady had answered Gianna, explaining to Gianna that the reason that she (Our Lady) looked so beautiful was because God was shining through her. I couldn't help but think that God's goodness was also shining through Mary Cook. From that moment I had no further doubts about her. If she was faking her apparitions, or if she had truly convinced herself that they were happening, when they were not, her response to me would have been different. If she was faking it, she would more likely feel threatened when I told her I was praying for her; if she had been convinced by Satan that these things were really happening, she would be offended that I was praying for her because, obviously, she was a very special person, so special that she didn't need anybodys' prayers!

From St. Maria Goretti Church, from a place where miracles of healing were happening, we went to one of God's greatest miracles, the Grand Canyon. It seemed a fitting place to end our pilgrimage. I was to see the fruits of our pilgrimage more than eight years later, when I learned that God had answered my spiritual petition! Another miracle, a miracle of Grace!

Because of the amazing impression these Lessons and messages had on me, I wanted to learn more and get some perspective on the source. So I went out and bought a couple of books on the apparitions in Scottsdale. One was titled *Our Lady Comes to Scottsdale, Is it Authentic?*, which was written by Robert Faricy, S.J. and Lucy Rooney, S.N.D. de N. The second book was titled *Our Lord and Our Lady in Scottsdale* by Father Rene Laurentin. Both books describe the happenings in Scottsdale in detail and give a brief history of the lives of the nine young adults who were involved in this story, and include photographs. What fascinated me was the fact that these visionaries came from all walks of life and that there seemed to be a relationship to Medjugorje.

When and how did the Scottsdale drama begin? The first public message from Our Lady to Dr. Gianna Talone occurred in Scottsdale on July 14, 1988. However, it could be said that the first stage of these events actually began much earlier with Susan Evans, one of the nine young visionaries involved in these happenings. As a child, Susan Evans had a dream of future chastisements and of Our Lord coming to the world with arms outstretched. Further, Our Blessed Mother had intimated to Susan that there would be apparitions in Scottsdale, AZ.

However, by the time Susan was 29 years old, she had grown lukewarm in her faith and had not been to church in seven months. In the fall of 1987 she suddenly heard Our Lord speak these words to her: "Pray to the Blessed Mother."[5] Later she heard "Would you suffer for me?"[6]; and then, when she said "Yes," Jesus asked her if she would be willing to suffer for others. Later, Jesus made it clear to Susan that she had been able to say yes only because He had given her the grace to do so. In November of 1987 Our Lady indicated that she wanted Susan to start a prayer group for the youth of the parish. This was the beginning of the prayer meetings for the young adults on Friday nights in St. Maria Goretti church in Scottsdale, an affluent section of Phoenix, AZ.

One month earlier, in September of 1987, Dr. Gianna Talone saw Mary in a dream. She tells Father Laurentin: "I awakened from sleep and was quite conscious that I had seen our Blessed Mother in front of me, a little to the right – a young slender woman dressed in a light white dress and veil."[7] This happened three nights in a row. Gianna goes on to say: "I would look at the Blessed Virgin and she would look at me. She did not talk but I felt a great peace in my heart – evidence that it was not a dream. I was sure of that. After this I experienced a great hunger for the Eucharist. I would go to Mass daily; I would pray long hours. I could hardly pull myself away from praying."[7]

In November 1987, as Gianna was praying during her lunch break, she had another very revealing experience. When she finished her prayers and was getting up to leave the Church she found that she could not get up. It was as if someone's hand was on her shoulder preventing her from rising. Then she heard a male voice saying "The Lord seeks favor upon you for you have cried for the Lord. You will do great things."[8]. These words disturbed her and she told no one, at the time, except her mother. It was only later that Our Lord was to tell her that it was the voice of the Angel Gabriel. Gianna also had a vision of eight young adults praying in front of Our Lady. Gianna was one of the eight. She recognized the others, although she did not know all of them by name, as parishioners of St. Maria Goretti. Later Gianna was to learn that each of these eight young adults, plus one more young man, was to play a special role in Our Lady's plan.

On December 3, 1987, a second prayer group was established by a number of these young adults in the parish after they returned from a pilgrimage to Medjugorje. It was known as Our Lady's Prayer Group. About 25 adults of varying ages were present at this first meeting. And it was at this first meeting that Gianna received her first locution. Subsequently, on July 14, 1988 Gianna received the first public message from the Blessed Virgin Mary during the Thursday Night Prayer meeting. Then on September 20, 1988, Gianna received her first Lesson from Our Lord intended for all of His people. This was a locution which Gianna had from Our Lord. It was not until Dec. 29, 1988, that Gianna had her first vision of Jesus. He came to her home as the Sacred Heart.

The pastor of St. Maria Goretti church at that time was Father Jack Spaulding, who had been ordained to the priesthood on June 5, 1971. His early work was with the deaf; and he learned, not only to use sign language, but also to say Mass using sign language. He was appointed Chancellor of the Diocese of Phoenix in 1980, and later Vicar Forane of the diocese being given responsibility for one-fourth of the diocese under the bishop. He was appointed pastor in 1982 of St. Maria Goretti, a church of approximately six thousand people. As part of his emphasis on spirituality, he had a Chapel built between the church and the parish office for perpetual adoration of the Blessed Sacrament. More than 700 parishioners signed-up for twenty-four hour adoration. Father Jack was also on the Board of Directors of St. John's Seminary in Camarillo, CA.

When the young adults first approached Fr. Jack about these mystical happenings, he was perplexed. He started to apply the traditional Catholic criteria in his evaluation of both the young adults and the happenings themselves. After initial and frequent doubts about the authenticity of these happenings, he came to the conclusion that God was working in his parish in a special way, that these were supernatural happenings. But he thought they were just for the benefit of the individuals themselves. So when Gianna came to him after the July 14, 1988 prayer meeting was ended and told him that she thought that she had received a message for the parish, he said to himself: "Oh, great, not only personal messages, but now public ones."[9]

As these events progressed, more than 500 people started showing up each week at St. Maria Goretti for Our Lady's Thursday night prayer meeting. During the meetings both Gianna and Annie Ross saw and heard Our Lady. Gianna writes the message down and then gives it to Fr. Jack to evaluate. If he is satisfied that the message is not contrary to Catholic teachings, he reads it at the next Thursday night meeting. However, he became concerned. He wondered whether he could control the situation and still successfully manage his large parish. In the book, Our *Lady of Emmitsburg,* he is quoted as thinking at the time that: "It was too big for him. He decided to isolate them from each other. He did not want them comparing notes. He was afraid that the situation might turn into a carnival-type event."[10] Fr. Jack says: "My problem was I was trying to control it….I went to my spiritual director who is versed in the early Fathers, and he said to me, 'Who are we to say that God can or can't act. We have to allow things to unfold in their timing.' I was trying to control the timing. I had to learn to let go – to say 'yes' to the Lord."[10]

The story of how the *I am your JESUS of MERCY* books came to be published gives an interesting insight into both Our Lady's and Fr. Jack's personalities. In August 1989, Gianna tells Fr. Jack that Our Lady told her that the Lessons from Our Lord were for the whole world; and should be published. Fr. Jack held off and did nothing about Our Lady's request. Our Lady then tells Gianna that: "you must continue to prod him until he relents."[11] Mary's motherly statement about continuing to prod Fr. Jack about this subject is a source of delight to me because it really shows how human Mary is! What Fr. Jack felt about Our Lady's request can be seen in Fr. Jack's answer to a question posed by Dom Forker, and reported in his book, *Our Lady of Emmitsburg, The Center of Her Immaculate Heart,* as follows:

> "Forker: Gianna said that you didn't initially believe her when she told you that Our Lady wanted Our Lord's messages to be published. Is that a fair account? Fr. Spaulding: I believed her. The messages were beautiful. I knew they were from Our Lord. But I didn't want to do it because I had a human fear. I had never published anything before, and I had a fear that if I published them, everything would blow up. So I said 'no.'"[12]

In 1987 Fr. Jack organized the Life Teen TV Program on EWTN. In connection with this TV show he went to Medjugorje to do a special show for the sixth anniversary of the first apparition. He was to return to Medjugorje four more times. On August 15, 1988, Father Jack was concelebrating the English-speaking Mass in Medjugorje. He indicates that it was very hot and that people were coming in and out of the church taking pictures while the Mass was being celebrated. After receiving Holy Communion, while waiting for others to finish distributing Communion, he was speaking to Our Lady. He said: "Dear Lady, you just can't be here any more. Look at these people, look at this – they have turned it into a carnival. You just can't be here still." Suddenly he heard a voice: "I am here, and I am going home with you."[13] At that same visit to Medjugorje, as he was walking from the Church of St. James to Vicka's house he heard these words: "You are to walk by faith and not by sight."[14] He was later to decide that these words meant that he was not to have any visions. This was the beginning of certain mystical phenomena which were to happen in Fr. Jack's life.

Fr. Laurentin points out in his book, *Our Lord and Our Lady in Scottsdale,* that the odd thing about Fr. Spaulding's position is: "not only is he the advised and respected authority, but he is also part of the special group. He considers himself as the tenth one."[15] The reason for this says Fr. Laurentin is that Fr. Jack: "became, much to his surprise, the echo of Jesus through his own homily."[15] According to Dom Forker: "One night in November, just before his homily, Fr. Jack blanked out as he was trying to speak. He could not even remember the Gospel that had just been read by the deacon. He felt drained. However, suddenly, he heard himself speaking. But it was not *him.* It was Our Lady speaking *through* him…One night in December, Fr. Spaulding realized the same sensations as he had that evening in November. But this time it was Our

Lord, not Our Lady, speaking through him. People who taped the homilies say the voice changes significantly from Our Lady to Our Lord."[16]

Fr. Jack states that he is never an "echo" of Our Lady or Our Lord, unless he says 'yes' to them. Fr. Jack is very honest about his feelings and seems to be well aware of his real motives. An example of these two points can be seen in a quote from Fr. Jack in the book, *Our Lady Comes to Scottsdale, Is it Authentic?* He says: "one time there were people I knew, visiting, in the congregation. I didn't want it to happen, but I felt it coming. I said 'no' and the feeling passed. Then I said, 'Lord do as you wish.' It happened."[17]

Gianna Talone was included as one of the eight visionaries that she had seen in a vision kneeling before Our Lady. Who is Gianna? What is her story? Gianna Talone was born on March 12, 1957 in Phoenix, Arizona. Her father, Jack, was born in Greenburgh, Pa. of Italian lineage. Her mother, Tecla was born in Italy and, at the time when she met and married Jack, she did not speak English and he did not speak Italian! When Gianna was born in a Catholic hospital, her mother was on the delivery table for eight hours. Gianna was a breach baby. According to Dom Forker: "The Catholic hierarchy of the hospital did not believe in Caesarian sections at the time. Finally, Tecla heard one of the nuns say, 'Sacrifice the mother and save the baby.'"[18] But her mother said: "'I'm not going to die, and neither is my baby.' Gianna was delivered with the cord around her neck. Later, as a result, Tecla had to have seven operations."[18] However, Tecla did not let this experience stop her from bringing her children up as Catholics. She took them regularly to Church on Sundays and holy days.

As Dom Forker writes, Gianna's father, Jack Talone "was a doer. He liked to see results. He became a millionaire from his dealings in real estate and mortgages, lost his money, and then bounced back to recover it."[19] He was concerned that his daughter get a good education. Gianna Talone graduated from Arizona State University in the spring of 1979. She received her Doctor of Pharmacy degree from the University of Southern California School of Pharmacy in Los Angeles. She did her internship at the UCLA Medical Center and her clerkships at Los Angeles and Culver City County hospitals. Dom Forker writes of Gianna that "Eighteen months later, on November 21, 1985, she married Michael Bianchi. The marriage lasted more than five years. During those years, she worked professionally as a director of pharmacy services, a vice-president of pharmacy services, a clinical pharmacist, a manager of a national drug formulary, a retail pharmacist, and a pharmacy coordinator."[20] In addition, she supported her husband during the first few years of their marriage.

Shortly after these supernatural happenings started, Gianna's life began to change and go downhill, not only at work but also in the Bianchi household. Michael Bianchi was not happy with the changes he saw in his wife. In addition, she was fired from her management position with a major pharmaceutical company on Dec. 30, 1988. As it turned out, her firing occurred on the very day, after she had her first apparition of Our Lord!

On New Year's Eve of Dec. 31, 1990: "Our Lady appeared to Gianna and said, 'The Eternal Father has granted your request. But your life will be different from this point on.' Two weeks later, Michael left her and filed for divorce. She has neither seen him nor heard from him since, except through his attorney."[21] There is no mention that I can find, as to what this request of Gianna's was, except that it was not for the divorce from Michael. It was a terrible shock for her because she loved her husband very much. However, he did not want children. She later learned that he even wrote this fact down during the Focus Exam required of couples preparing for marriage in the Diocese of Phoenix. After her conversion, Gianna stopped using contraceptives, and

Michael broke off sexual relations with her. Our Lady told Gianna that she would get an annulment in eight months, although it usually takes two years in the Phoenix Diocese. Eight months to the day, Gianna got her annulment!

Even before the divorce, things continued to get worse financially for Gianna. The only job she could get at the time was as a pharmacist, working twelve-hour shifts at a Walgreens Drugstore, two blocks from St. Maria Goretti Church. Then, through the intercession of St. Joseph, she got a position as a clinical pharmacist at St. Joseph's Hospital. She worked her way up to pharmacy coordinator of a 250-bed Nursing Home Care Unit just being opened by the Hospital. However, this new job did not resolve her financial difficulties. It all started to become too much for her and she experienced escalating anxiety which was partly related to the problems in her marriage and partly the stress of her new position and lingering financial problems. The effect on her was such that her physician told her to take a six-month leave of absence from her job at St. Joseph's Hospital.

Shortly after she returned to her job at St. Joseph's Hospital, after her six-month leave was over, she lost her job and was unable to meet her mortgage payments on her small condominium. The professional world to which she had belonged started to black-ball her. The only work that she could get was part-time. Except for one non-Catholic friend, all of her former friends deserted Gianna. She was in such financial straights that she finally came to the point where she could not pay her electric bill. However, her lights were not turned off because an unknown benefactor paid the bill. Another benefactor left food stamps that they purchased from a local grocery. She also had detractors. A priest in Arizona claimed: "that at one time he was her spiritual director. In truth, however, he was not. Claiming that she is diabolical, he excoriates her in his homilies and on his pilgrimages. He has even prayed 'over her' for exorcism."[22]

All during this time of severe trials, Gianna continued to receive Lessons from Jesus.

In November of 1992 a major change in Gianna's life was to begin. As if to reassure Gianna regarding the trials she had endured, Jesus gives Gianna a Lesson on faith. On Nov. 27, 1992, He tells Gianna and all of us that: "when your feelings are lost, when you have no desire for God because you are constrained and your will is arid, *when you think you are incapable of spiritual advancement, know you are in a healthy place.*"[23] I found this particular Lesson which Jesus identifies as being on spirituality, very enlightening. He makes a thought-provoking statement. Jesus says that the signs, as well as the spiritual experiences which He gives us are intended to take us away from ourselves! Jesus also explains that He wishes to bring each of us "to fulfillment by a way that I have designed specifically for you…I call all to a deep dimension of faith because this is where true union with God exists. This is where you ascend in prayer. The Church does not place too much weight on illumined experiences for this reason. Faith is a movement. It is the living faith which allows you to make progress moving from the finite world into the infinite Being of God."[23]

This Lesson was to be the last one Gianna would receive for the next two years. But this is not the major change in Gianna Talone's life of which I speak. Although in a way it could be seen as being related to what happened. In November, Gianna met Dr. Michael Sullivan. He was a physician with a lucrative practice. But he felt that something was missing. He was seeking God's will in his life. During a prayer service in Gianna's home at which Mike was present, Our Lady appeared to Gianna and said: "Allow me to introduce you to your new husband."[24] After they began their courtship, Mike took Gianna to the Grotto of Lourdes in Emmitsburg, Maryland, a special place for him. This was January 31, 1993. During their visit there Our

Lady appeared to Gianna and invited her and Mike to move to Emmitsburg after their marriage.

On March 25, 1993, the Feast of the Annunciation, they left for Europe to make a private retreat, beginning in Assisi and ending in Medjugorje. Just before they left Our Lady appeared to Gianna and told her: “Satan does not want this marriage. He has been given free reign during this period to disrupt it. You will be tempted to call it off, but I don’t want you to make a decision about this marriage until after Easter Sunday.”[25] According to Michael: “The retreat turned out to be ‘six weeks of pure hell.’”[25] Finally, one night, Gianna could take it no longer and she called off the marriage. However, the Lord and Padre Pio intervened and Gianna relented. They were married on June 19, 1993, the Feast of the Immaculate Heart of Mary. They moved to Emmitsburg on November 1, 1993.

At some point Our Blessed Mother indicated that she wished that, each of the nine young adults who were involved in the supernatural happenings in Scottsdale, would make a special commitment to her for three years. During that period they were not to get married, or enter a seminary or religious community. When I originally read this, I wondered what it was all about. But now it seems to me that Our Lady was forming them spiritually so that they would be able to assist the Mother of God in her Plan. In a message given by Jesus to the Thursday Night Prayer Group He says: “You live as if you have not said yes! Say ‘yes’ again this night. Please, believe when I say to you, your ‘yes’ is crucial to My plan, which is My mother’s plan.”[26]

As I look back now, it seems to me that the first step in Mary’s plan was to start a series of prayer groups. Susan Evans was one of the nine. As indicated above, as the result of a locution she received from the Blessed Mother, she started the Friday Night Prayer Group in the fall of 1987 with the help of Stephanie Staab. Then Wendy Nelson and her brother, Steve, as well as Mary Cook joined the group. Then Our Lady's Thursday night prayer group was formed. All of these young adults were identified in Gianna's vision as being part of the nine adults selected for a special mission.

In addition to Susan Evans and Gianna Talone, who are the remaining seven young adults? What is their story? They are a disparate group, coming from different backgrounds and interests. Most of them have had mystical experiences, generally in the form of locutions but also, at times, these experiences include apparitions of Jesus and Mary. Some of them receive messages from either Jesus or Mary for the world or for individual participants during the weekly prayer meetings. All of them seem to have undergone a profound metanoia. Background information on the remaining seven is provided below.

Stefanie Staab graduated from the University of Arizona in 1987 with a major in finance and accounting. Her religion did not play a major role in her life until, at the age of 25, she witnessed the conversion of a co-worker and began to take stock of her own relationship to God. Shortly thereafter she helped to start the young adult prayer group with Susan Evans. She receives locutions both from Jesus and Mary.

Wendy Nelson, a student at the Arizona State University, started going to the Thursday Night Prayer Group as the result of her mother's encouragement. One day she heard an interior voice say: "Would you give up everything for Me?"[27] Wendy responded that she would, believing that it was Jesus who spoke to her. Wendy says that before this happened "I would not go to Mass unless I felt like it, more or less once a month. I was not happy. I was searching."[27] She says that her life has changed and that she now goes to daily Mass.

Wendy's brother, Steve, was in his mid-twenties pursuing his goal of becoming "world champion calf roper and steer wrestler"[28] when his conversion began. He felt as if

Jesus and Mary were speaking to him in his heart. He decided that he had to choose between the sport of roping and God. He choose God. As a result he started to participate in the young adult prayer group, to go to daily Mass, and to fast on Wednesdays and Fridays.

Mary Cook was working as a traveling salesperson when she decided to go to Medjugorje. While there she felt that she had to change her life. She returned home and began to read the messages from Medjugorje. She felt drawn to "live them."[29] She began to receive locutions from Jesus and Mary. Later she started receiving messages during the young adult prayer meeting on Fridays.

Annie Ross had given up her university studies and gotten a job as a real estate agent in order to help her husband, a Turkish Muslim, continue his studies. Annie relates that on March 31, 1989 during the Thursday Night Prayer meeting Our Lady asked her: "Do you want to give me your heart? You must make the decision either for me or against. It is your decision to give it to me or not?"[30] Annie responded positively. Since then she has received locutions both from Jesus and from Mary.

In 1985 Jimmy Kupanoff went with his family and his girlfriend to Medjugorje. He made a second pilgrimage in 1987 during which time God's presence made a strong impression on him. Both he and his family began to change and were drawn to a more prayerful life. He began to attend the Friday Night Prayer Group. He has received interior locutions both from Our Lord and from Our Lady.

James Pauley was the youngest in the group of nine. His conversion began in 1985 during a retreat conducted by Father Spaulding. He explains: "I experienced a profound presence of God – that He exists and that He loves me. From this point on my life was different."[31]

What was the plan of the Blessed Mother? How did these nine young adults fit into this plan? When I first read the *I am your JESUS of MERCY* books I was not focusing on these questions. What impressed me most powerfully were the Lessons from Jesus. They present a complete treatise on the spiritual journey. They start with the basic Christian teachings and slowly build until they present the most advanced spiritual themes of the journey of the soul to God. And what was of particular importance to me personally was the emphasis these Lessons placed on mystical contemplation.

SEVEN

SPIRITUAL MARRIAGE

I have tried to analyze why I always seemed to feel so uncomfortable and defensive about my lifelong interest in mystical contemplation. As I did so I found that my attitudes had slowly changed over the years since I took early retirement from my career as an engineer. Some of the things that bothered me included the nature of mysticism and the terminology employed by Christian mystics; my personal prejudices and biases towards mystical phenomena such as visions and locutions; and finally the attitudes prevalent in the culture in which I am a part.

How does mystical contemplation fit into Christian spirituality? And is it part of the traditional development of things of the Spirit? The *Catechism of the Catholic Church* summarizes Christian spirituality this way: "The Christian tradition comprises three major expressions of the life of prayer: vocal prayer, meditation, and contemplative prayer. They have in common the recollection of the heart." (Catechism #2721) In this context, the term meditation refers to *discursive* meditation rather than the silent meditation of the East.

There are only two pages on contemplative prayer in the *Catechism* and consequently mystical contemplation is not addressed in any depth. However, it is a very good summary. In particular, I liked the following paragraph: "Contemplative prayer is the simplest expression of the mystery of prayer. It is a *gift*, a grace; it can be accepted only in humility and poverty. Contemplative prayer is a *covenant* relationship established by God within our hearts. Contemplative prayer is a *communion* in which the Holy Trinity conforms man, the image of God, 'to his likeness.'" (Catechism #2713)

The Reverend Adolphe Tanquerey, S.S., D.D., indicates that he wrote his textbook, *The Spiritual Life*, primarily for priests and seminarians. It was from this book I first learned about Christian spirituality. I began to read it in Mt. St. Mary's Abbey when I started to encounter, what I considered, difficulties in prayer. It is interesting to see in what different terms the spiritual life is presented herein, as compared to the quotes from the *Catholic Catechism*, which I used above. In item No. 340, Fr. Tanquerey discusses the fact that there are many stages, or degrees of perfection in this life. However, he writes that: "there are three *principal stages*, or as they are commonly called, *three ways:* that of *beginners* – the purgative way, that of souls already *advanced* – the illuminative way, and that of the *perfect* – the unitive way." I was surprised to learn that this terminology goes back to St. Thomas, a preeminent Doctor of the Church.

St. John of the Cross incorporates the writings of St. Thomas in his books on mystical contemplation. Later in this chapter you will see how John of the Cross mentions these three ways, the purgative, the illuminative and unitive, when he explains the theme of his book, the *Spiritual Canticle*, which is based on the *Song of Songs* from Sacred Scripture. I will not go into a discussion of these three ways since it is fully and beautifully covered in the works of St. John of the Cross.

However, I do want to bring up one topic. That is relative to what John of the Cross means when he uses the terminology, *night of sense* and *night of spirit,* which are commonly referred to as the *Dark Nights*, which one encounters on the mystical journey. John of the Cross explains what he means when he speaks of dark nights in the very first chapter of his famous work, *Ascent of Mount Carmel*. He relates them to the three ways I discussed above. He says that both nights are periods of purgation, the first relates to the sensual and the second relates to the spiritual parts of the soul. The night of sense occurs when the soul is advancing in the beginner state of the spiritual life. He makes a very important point. John of the Cross says that the Lord uses the night of sense to initiate the beginner into the contemplative state! He says that the night of spirit is encountered by advanced souls when Our Lord desires to bring them into the unitive state. It is the commonly accepted teaching that when the night of spirit is over, the soul reaches the state of transforming union with the Triune God, or as is sometimes expressed, the soul becomes the bride of Christ in the *Spiritual Marriage.*

It seemed to me that most people looked upon mysticism as an esoteric subject. In the Catholic Church I knew, mystical experiences belonged to the world of the saints rather than to the every day Catholic. As a matter of fact there was a debate going on among those who wrote about the spiritual life as to whether contemplation was part of the normal progression of spiritual development, that is, whether there was a "universal call" to contemplation or whether it was a path reserved only for the few.

I first learned of this debate in reading one of Garrigou-Lagrange's books. I don't remember the name of the book but he was one of the few writers at the time who was on the side of the universal call. I spent much time reading this particular book because it provided a beautiful and comprehensive study of the fruits of contemplation in our daily life. However, since this issue of a universal call was not settled, I continued questioning my right to be so interested in contemplative prayer. It was not until I became acquainted with Abbot Thomas Keating's books and the organization he founded, Contemplative Outreach, that this issue of a 'universal call' was finally resolved to my satisfaction.

One thing that made me feel on the defensive and uncomfortable in discussing mystical contemplation was the erotic terminology often used in expressing mystical concepts. The use of the term spiritual marriage is a good example of this. When I did talk about mysticism, I made a point of using the expression "transforming union" rather than spiritual marriage. I can remember once using the word's spiritual marriage at one of our Centering Prayer gatherings and observing that one of the men present looked very uncomfortable. That only added to my desire not to use such terminology. The irony of this is that when I became a nun, I was called the bride of Christ. I wore a wedding gown and veil as I took my first vows as a Trappistine. This was so traditional and so much a part of our Catholic culture at the time that it did not bother me at all!

But I would sometimes muse as to why God would use such symbols, particularly those used in the Biblical book, the *Song of Songs* (*Canticle of Canticles*). I got a better insight when I read Lawrence Boadt's book, *Reading the Old Testament*. With reference to the *Song of Songs*, he writes: "But the lusty nature of the songs gave scandal to many of the Jewish rabbis, and as late as the second century A.D. they still had not fully agreed that the book should be in the sacred canon. One of the deciding factors was the belief that it described allegorically the love of Yahweh for Israel as a beloved bride. The Christian Church accepted it quickly for the same reasons – it could easily describe in allegory the love of Christ for the Church, or for the soul of the believer. St. Bernard of Clairvaux in the twelfth century wrote a great number of sermons on the *Song of Songs*, describing the love of Christ for the soul and the mystical union that came from this love. They have become the classic source of such a mystical spirituality."[1]

St. Bernard, who was a Cistercian Abbot, and also a Doctor of the Church, based his sermons on the first two chapters and the first verse of the third chapter of the *Songs*. In Evelyn Underhill's *The Mystics of the Church,* she writes with reference to Bernard's sermons on the *Songs*: "Imagery of this kind is apt to displease modern readers, who seldom possess the shining purity of soul which safeguarded those who first employed it. But his metaphors cannot obscure the simplicity, sanity and depth of Bernard's mysticism."[2] I suspect that Evelyn Underhill in referring to "modern readers" probably meant modern "religiously inclined" readers. I hardly think it likely that the average American today can be shocked by anything sexual.

I found a particularly interesting insight into the impact of St. Bernard's emphasis on nuptial mysticism in Carol Lee Flinder's book *Enduring Grace.* She is speaking of St. Bernard's famous commentary on the *Song of Songs*. Carol Lee Flinder highlights the impact of Bernard's writings in this way: "Bernard's teaching brought a new and powerfully attractive metaphor into play. Dwelling in turn upon each hauntingly beautiful line of the text ["Strengthen me with flagons, and comfort me with apples, for I am sick of love."], he moved beyond the traditional interpretation, wherein the bridegroom was Christ and the bride the Church, and urged the monks under his direction to consider *themselves* the brides of Christ – to anoint and bejewel themselves inwardly and ready themselves in every way for the kiss of Christ – for the experience, that is, of mystical union with God."[3] I wonder how the monks felt about this emphasis on their "bejeweling" themselves as brides of Christ! Obviously they were very receptive to it as witnessed by Bernard's popularity and the growth of the Cistercian order at that time.

St. John of the Cross, following on the tradition of St. Bernard, wrote the *Spiritual Canticle* which was patterned after the *Song of Songs*. This book expounds on his poem "Stanzas Between the Soul and the Bridegroom," most of which he wrote while he was imprisoned in a dungeon in Toledo by the Calced Carmelite friars. Interestingly enough, he was persuaded to write the commentary on the stanzas by a woman, Mother Ann of Jesus, who was prioress of the Discalced Carmelite nuns at the time.

What is the difference between the 'Calced' and 'Discalced' Carmelites? And more importantly, why and how was John of the Cross imprisoned by the Calced Carmelite friars? Webster's Dictionary defines 'calced' by stating that "it is used of religious who wear shoes." It is a fascinating read as to how the word discalced, when applied to the Carmelites, came to designate that branch of the Carmelites who went without shoes as a sign of austerity. The Discalced Carmelites were a reform group of Carmelites, founded by St. Teresa of Avila and St. John of the Cross. They are sometimes referred to as the Teresian Carmelites. In the 16th century, the Calced Carmelites, who were permitted to wear shoes, lived according to the mitigated rule of St. Simon Stock.

John of the Cross first met St. Teresa when he went to Medina del Campo to sing his first Mass. While they talked, he mentioned that he planned to leave the Carmelites for the more austere life of the Carthusians. Mother Teresa was in Medina del Campo to complete her second foundation of Carmelite Nuns of the Reform, which she had initiated. Fr. John had been recommended to her and she was obviously impressed for she immediately urged him to stay in the Carmelites and help her to establish the Reform among the friars. John of the Cross agreed to help her.

The story of the relationship between the Calced and Discalced Carmelites is long and complicated. However, I will briefly mention how Fr. John came to be imprisoned in Toledo by the Calced Carmelite friars because it provides an interesting insight into the keen mind of John of the Cross and the politics involved in the situation.

At the time of his capture and imprisonment, Fr. John was stationed at the Discalced Carmelite foundation of the Incarnation. He was assigned there by the Papal Nuncio, at the express request of the nuns of the Incarnation, despite the fact that Fr. John's position at the Incarnation was coveted by the Calced friars. When the Nuncio died, things changed. Fr. John was ordered to leave, return to a Calced monastery, and renounce the Reform as required by the Chapter at Piacenza, Italy, in May 1575. However, Fr. John had a legal mind, and he realized that they did not have jurisdiction over him since he had been appointed by the Papal Nuncio and the appointment was still in effect. He therefore refused their request. Either they missed the nuisance involved in John of the Cross' argument or they didn't believe them. As a result, the Calced superior disbursed a number of friars, together with men-at-arms (their use was legal at the time) to capture and imprison John of the Cross.

In his *Canticle* which he wrote during his imprisonment, John of the Cross explains the theme of his work as follows: "These stanzas begin with a person's initial steps in the service of God and continue until he reaches spiritual marriage, the ultimate state of perfection. They refer, consequently, to the three states or ways of spiritual exercise [purgative, illuminative and unitive] through which a person passes in his advance to this state, and they describe some of the characteristics and effects of these ways."[4] Further on he says: "The soul does not come to this garden of complete transformation [which is the joy and delight and glory of the Spiritual Marriage] without first passing through the Spiritual Betrothal and through the mutual and loyal love of those that are betrothed."[5]

In speaking of this betrothal, John of the Cross writes these beautiful and amazing words: "In this interior union God communicates Himself to the soul with such genuine love that no mother's affection, in which she tenderly caresses her child, nor brother's love, nor friendship is comparable to it. The tenderness and truth of love by which the immense Father favors and exalts this humble and loving soul reaches such a degree – O wonderful thing, worthy of all our awe and admiration – that the Father Himself becomes subject to her for her exaltation, as though He were her servant and she His lord. And He is as solicitous in favoring her as He would be if He were her slave and she His god. So profound is the humility and sweetness of God!"[6]

St Teresa of Avila also wrote about the *Song of Songs* in her *Conceptions of the Love of God.*. Feminist historians of religion would not be surprised at these words from Father-Master Fray Jeronimo Gracian's Introduction to the Conceptions: "Among the books which she wrote was one containing Divine conceptions and loftiest thoughts on the love of God, on prayer and on other heroic virtues, in which were expounded many words from the *Songs of Solomon.* But one of her confessors, thinking it a new and dangerous thing that a woman should write on the *Songs* ordered this book to be burned."[7] This fact was verified during the course of the Beatification and Canonization of St. Teresa by Maria de San Jose who stated that Father Master Fray Diego de Yanguas, upon seeing the book Teresa had written on the *Songs*, ordered that it be burned because as he said "it did not seem suitable to him that a woman should write on the Songs."[8] Teresa obeyed immediately. Lucky for us, some of the sisters had copies which Teresa did not know about and which were preserved during the ensuing centuries.

In commenting on the *Song of Songs*, Teresa writes in her colloquial way how some people reacted to the words employed in the Songs: "You may think that in these *Canticles* there are some things which might have been said in a different way. We are so stupid that I should not be surprised if you did; I have heard some people say that they actually tried not to listen to them."[9] She could have been talking about me! Further on she writes: "I remember, once upon a time, hearing a religious preach a most admirable sermon, the greater part of which was a description of the joys that result from the Bride's converse with God; and the people laughed so much and so completely misinterpreted what he said, for he was speaking of love…that I was astounded."[10] This is the other thing that bothered me, that people might either be shocked at the mystic's use of erotic language or smile condescendingly. I do not know which bothered me more!

However, as I write this chapter, I find that my attitude has completely changed. It now seems to me that God is trying to impress on us the fact that the transforming union is a true, not symbolic, union between God and the soul. And, just as the birth of a child into the world is the ultimate union between husband and wife, likewise, at the final resurrection, the transforming union of the mystic culminates in "Christ's transfiguration of our bodies."[11] It is a new rebirth in which our bodies are changed and as St. Peter indicates, Jesus our Lord has promised that we will "come to share in the very being of God." (2 Peter 1:4) This is the beatitude to which God calls us!

In the Spiritual Canticle John of the Cross speaks of the spiritual marriage as having already occurred [12] and he talks about consummation of this marriage. I had always assumed that he meant consummation in this life. However, he writes: "**when** the Spiritual Marriage between God and the soul is consummated, there are two natures in one spirit and one love of God."[13](emphasis mine) Note the use of the word "when" which can be interpreted as future tense. That is, not yet consummated. This interpretation is confirmed by John of the Cross in the *Living Flame of Love*, where he has the soul pray, that if it be God's will, that He "Perfect and consummate the spiritual marriage in me with the beatific vision of Thyself."[14]

I now feel that the use of the term, spiritual marriage, is far richer and more descriptive than the words transforming union. And it seems very appropriate to me that God should describe the spiritual union between Himself and a soul in terms of the bride and the Bridegroom. But when I was younger, I simply couldn't understand why God would use marriage and the erotic images of the *Songs* to describe His relationship with us. It embarrassed me. I realize now that I was trying to tell God: **how to be God!!!** The same was true of my reactions to visions, locutions, etc. as I will discuss in the next chapter.

EIGHT

MYSTICAL PHENOMENA

As I mentioned in the previous chapter, my reactions to mystical contemplation were also affected by my personal prejudices and biases towards mystical phenomena such as visions or apparitions and locutions. As the soul commences the contemplative journey, it may begin to experience such things. It was not clear to me whether they were an integral part of contemplation or not.

St. Teresa of Avila wrote one of the most famous books on mystical contemplation ever written, which she called the *Interior Castle*. In a conversation with Fray Diego in which she describes how she came to write this book, St. Teresa told him how she wanted to get some insight into the beauty of the soul in grace. She then told him that just before she started to write God gave her the following vision:

> "He showed her a most beautiful crystal globe, made in the shape of a castle, and containing seven mansions, in the seventh and innermost of which was the King of Glory, in the greatest splendor, illumining and beautifying them all. The nearer one got to the center, the stronger was the light; outside the palace limits everything was foul, dark and infested with toads, vipers and other venomous creatures."[1]

In writing the actual words of the *Interior Castle*, St. Teresa first describes the vision referenced above, although she does not say it was a vision that she had, because she was trying to avoid further contact with the Inquisition who were then examining her previous book. In the course of describing each mansion, St. Teresa writes a great deal about raptures, ecstasy, flights of the spirit, intellectual visions and imaginary visions. I will let Teresa describe these phenomena in her own words because she does it so well.

In Chapter III of the Sixth Mansion of the *Interior Castle*, Teresa speaks of God's awakening of the soul via locutions, of which she says: "Some of them (locutions) seem to come from without; others from the innermost depths of the soul; others from its highest part; while others, again, are so completely outside the soul that they can be heard with the ears, and seem to be uttered by a human voice."[2] She goes on to comment that "these may come from God, in any of the ways I have mentioned, or they may equally well come from the devil or from one's own imagination."[3] In the rest of the chapter she expounds on all of these phenomena and tells how one is to know if they are from God, the devil or the imagination. It is an excellent chapter for anyone interested in understanding locutions, particularly with regard to similar things experienced by the visionaries of our era.

In Chapter IV, she describes a kind of rapture wherein the soul "is struck by some word, which it either remembers or hears spoken by God. His Majesty is moved with compassion at having seen the soul suffering so long through its yearning for Him and…God unites it with Himself, in a way which none can understand save it and He, and even the soul itself does not understand this in such a way as to be able to speak of it afterwards, though it is not deprived of its interior senses;…The position, in this case, as I understand it, is that the soul has never before been so fully awake to the things of God or had such light or such knowledge of His Majesty. This may seem impossible because, if the faculties are so completely absorbed that we might describe them as dead, and the senses are so as well, how can the soul be said to understand this secret? I cannot say, nor perhaps can any creature, but only the Creator Himself."[4] She continues to describe this and similar experiences in the next few chapters.

In Chapter VIII of the Sixth Mansion, St. Teresa gives a very good explanation of intellectual visions in her own inimitable and colloquial manner. She explains that this vision is different from an imaginary vision in that, while one knows that the vision of the person is a reality, one does not see this vision either with one's own physical eyes or with one's imagination. Yet you somehow know who it is, whether it is Our Lord, Our Lady or another person. In addition, St. Teresa adds a very interesting statement to the effect that, relative to previous locutions which she had experienced, it was not until she had this intellectual vision that she knew that the person who had been talking to her was Jesus Christ Our Lord!

It is difficult to understand what St. Teresa is saying here unless one connects it to the earlier chapter on locutions. In that chapter St. Teresa says that: "There is another way in which the Lord speaks to the soul, which for my own part I hold to be very certainly genuine, and that is by a kind of intellectual vision,"[5] She goes on to speak very highly of this type of locution.

St. Teresa makes another interesting observation relative to the time that this intellectual vision may last. She indicates that the vision can last for days, months or even as much as a year. Later, when I write about St. Teresa's description of imaginary visions you will learn that they, by comparison, last only a very short period of time.

In reading the following quotation from St. Teresa on intellectual visions it should be noted that when St. Teresa writes "I saw a person," she is actually speaking of herself. Here is what she says:

> "It may happen that, while the soul is not in the least expecting Him to be about to grant it this favor, which it has never thought it can possibly deserve, it is conscious that Jesus Christ Our Lord is near to it, though it cannot see Him either with the eyes of the body or with those of the soul. This [I do not know why] is called an intellectual vision. I saw a person to whom God had granted this favor,....She had never heard of an intellectual vision, or realized that there was any such thing, but she understood quite clearly that it was this Lord Who often spoke to her in the way I have described (see above paragraph on locutions): until He granted her this favor to which I am referring she never knew Who was speaking to her, although she understood the words.
>
> "Being frightened about this vision, for it is not like an imaginary vision, which is quickly gone, but lasts for many days – sometimes for more than a year, she went off to her confessor in a state of great perturbation. 'If you see nothing,' he asked, 'how do you know it is Our Lord?' Then he told her to tell him what His face was like. She replied that she did not know, that she had seen no face, and that she could not tell him more than she had done already: what she did know was that it was He Who was speaking to her and it was no fancy."[6]

St. Teresa concludes the chapter with an important admonition for her sisters. She makes it quite clear that while mystical phenomena can lead us to God, that it is often given to the sisters most in need of such consolations. She says: "And let none of you imagine that, because a sister has had such experiences, she is any better than the rest; the Lord leads each of us as He sees we have need. Such experiences, if we use them aright, prepare us to be better servants of God; but sometimes it is the weakest whom God leads by this road. And so there is no ground here either for approval or for condemnation. We must base our judgments on the virtues. The saintliest will be she who serves Our Lord with the greatest mortification and humility and purity of conscience."[7]

St. Teresa begins Chapter IX by discussing how the Lord communicates Himself to the soul through an imaginary vision. She makes an interesting case for the idea that imaginary visions are actually more profitable than intellectual visions! When Dr. Gianna Sullivan goes into ecstasy and sees Our Blessed Mother almost every night except Friday, she is probably experiencing the type of imaginary vision described by St. Teresa. Notice that St. Teresa says that this type of vision, unlike intellectual visions, only lasts for a very short time, probably on the order of minutes. As a matter of fact she indicates that: "When the soul is able to remain for a long time looking upon the Lord, I do not think it can be a vision at all."[8]

Although St. Teresa is speaking about an imaginary vision of Jesus which she experienced, I think that her words can also be applied to Our Blessed Mother. Here is what St. Teresa says:

> "Let us now come to imaginary visions, in which the devil is said to interfere more frequently than in those (intellectual visions) already described. This may well be the case; but when they come from Our Lord they seem to me in some way more profitable because they are in closer conformity with our nature, except for those which the Lord bestows in the final Mansion, and with which no others can compare....
>
> "When Our Lord is pleased to bestow greater consolations upon this soul, He grants it, in whatever way He thinks best, a clear revelation of His sacred Humanity, either as He was when He lived in the world, or as He was after His resurrection; and although He does this so quickly that we might liken

> the action to a flash of lightning, this most glorious image is so deeply engraved upon the imagination that I do not believe it can possibly disappear until it is seen where it can be enjoyed in all eternity.
>
> "I speak of an 'image', but it must not be supposed that one looks at it as at a painting; it is really alive, and sometimes even speaks to the soul and shows it things both great and secret. But you must realize that, although the soul sees this for a certain length of time, it can no more be gazing at it all the time than it could keep gazing at the sun. So the vision passes very quickly..."[9]

In the Seventh Mansion, St. Teresa speaks of the transforming union and stresses that the reason God grants this grace is so that the soul's "whole thought will be concentrated upon finding ways to please Him and upon showing Him how it loves Him. This, my daughters, is the aim of prayer: this is the purpose of the Spiritual Marriage, of which are born good works and good works alone."[10] In this mansion St. Teresa speaks not only of intellectual visions but also of imaginary visions which may occur at this point. Actually, St. Teresa seems to imply that an intellectual vision is necessary to usher a soul into the Seventh Mansion! In writing in the first chapter of the Seventh and last mansion, St. Teresa says that the soul: "is brought into this Mansion by means of an intellectual vision, in which, by a representation of the truth in a particular way, the Most Holy Trinity reveals Itself, in all three Persons."[11]

Then in the next chapter, St. Teresa begins to discuss in detail the Spiritual Marriage which occurs in the Seventh Mansion. She speaks of an imaginary vision that takes place during the Spiritual Marriage. However, she adds a caveat of sorts at the end. St. Teresa in writing about the "Divine and Spiritual Marriage," says: "When granting this favor for the first time, His Majesty is pleased to reveal Himself to the soul through an imaginary vision of His most sacred Humanity, so that it may clearly understand what is taking place and not be ignorant of the fact that it is receiving so sovereign a gift. To other people the experience will come in a different way."[12]

If I am interpreting St. Teresa correctly in that she seems to imply that an intellectual vision and probably, an imaginary vision are required for the soul to reach the transforming union, then visions are indeed an integral part of contemplation! For a long time, this was one of my questions about contemplation and the mystical marriage, whether one could be in the state of union with God, that is, the transforming union, without ever having experienced the visions that St. Teresa describes? Besides St. Teresa, what do other writers on mystical contemplation have to say about this question?

In the *Ascent of Mt. Carmel*, St. John of the Cross describes what he means when he writes about the union of the soul with God. He points out that God is present substantially in every soul, no matter whether he is sinner or saint! This union is wrought by the fact that God is continuously preserving us in existence. Without this moment to moment support we would cease to be. In contrast to this type of union, John of the Cross is speaking of a supernatural union in which "when the soul rids itself totally of that which is repugnant to the Divine will…it is transformed in God through love."[13]

In explaining how the soul is brought to this union by God (for it is God who really does the work, not the soul), he explains why God gives the soul supernatural experiences through the senses. He writes: "In order that God lift the soul from the extreme of its low state to the other extreme of the high state of divine union," God must start "by touching the low state and extreme of the senses. And from there He must gradually bring the soul *after its own manner* to the other end, spiritual wisdom, which is incomprehensible to the senses…This is the reason God gives a person visions, forms, images and other sensitive and spiritual knowledge…not because He does not desire to give spiritual wisdom immediately, in the first act."[14] (italics mine)

Surprisingly, John of the Cross goes on to say that the soul must not receive them! In his words: "when there is a question of imaginative visions or other supernatural communications apprehensible by the senses and independent of a man's free will, I affirm that at whatever season, [in the state of perfection or one less perfect], an individual must not desire to give them admittance, even though they come from God."[15] These words are very difficult to understand unless one carefully examines them in the context of John of the Cross' other writings. This subject is discussed further in my chapter on Mystical Contemplation.

Writing two centuries before John of the Cross and Teresa, the anonymous author (thought to be English) of the *Cloud of Unknowing* speaks of contemplation, but does not address extraordinary phenomena such as visions, etc., except in Chapter 71. It is an interesting chapter, not only in that he speaks of contemplative ecstasy, but in what he says of it relative to the transforming union. He says that there are some people who believe that perfect contemplation is only experienced at "rare moments of ecstasy called ravishing."[16] He says that, to the contrary, that "God, in his wisdom, determines the course and the character of each one's contemplative journey" and that there are some "so spiritually refined by grace and so intimate with God in prayer that they seem to possess and experience the perfection of this work (contemplation) almost as they like, even in the midst of their ordinary daily routine…"[16]

The author of the *Cloud of Unknowing* discusses the *work* of contemplation in great detail and points out the key point of contemplation as follows: "Rational creatures such as men and angels possess two principal faculties, a knowing power and a loving power. No one can fully comprehend the uncreated God with his knowledge; but each one, in a different way, can grasp him fully through love."[17] Later on in a chapter on Luke's Gospel, he discusses the story of Martha and Mary, wherein Our Lord tells Martha: "Martha, Martha, you are fretting and fussing about so many things; but one thing is necessary. The part that Mary has chosen is best; and it shall not be taken away from her." (Luke 10:41-42) In discussing this story, he explains the function of the *cloud of unknowing* as follows: "there never has been and there never will be a creature so pure or so deeply immersed in the loving contemplation of God who does not approach him in this life through that lofty and marvelous *cloud of unknowing*."[18]

In my copy of the *Cloud of Unknowing* published by Image Books in 1973, there is an exceptionally good Introduction relative to the nature and theology of contemplation by Father William Johnston. In the very first paragraph he expounds on the importance of mysticism in our era and he relates it to the mysticism of the East. He further points out that in this age of anxiety, our world needs mystical contemplation now in a way that it never has in the past. He writes:

> "Recent times have witnessed a revival of interest in Western mysticism. It is as though the West, long exposed to Zen and Yoga and the spiritual systems of the East, now searches for its own tradition and its own spiritual heritage. Strangely enough, the interest in mysticism is not just academic. It is also practical. Many people are anxious to read the mystics in order to practice the doctrine they teach and to experience the states of consciousness they depict. In short, interest in Christian mysticism is part of a widespread craving for meditation, for contemplation, for depth –

> a desire to get beyond the changing phenomena and the future shock and the global village into a deeper reality that lies at the center of things. **Mysticism is no longer irrelevant; it is in the air we breathe."**[19] (emphasis mine)

Relative to the nature of mysticism and the East-West religious encounter Fr. Johnston emphasizes that while much has been written in the western world about meditation, the west usually addresses discursive meditation, rather than eastern meditation which goes beyond words and images. We often look to how others use words about God when we want to understand their religious persuasion. For example, I found a new insight into Pope John Paul II's spirituality when I read the Mass card published by the Camden Diocese for Pope John following his death. It read:

> "And yet I do not altogether die,
> "what is indestructible in me remains!...
> "What is imperishable in me
> "now stands face to face before Him Who Is!"

I often think that many people are unaware of this aspect of Catholic belief, that words cannot express who we are or who God is. For it is all mystery. The God we Catholics believe in is the **I am** of Sacred Scripture. God is essentially unknowable to our intellects in this life and that is why the English author of the *Cloud* writes of the *cloud of unknowing*. Fr. Johnston compares the *cloud of unknowing* to the *silentium mysticum* of Dionysius. This is what Fr. Johnston has to say: "While there is an abundance of books teaching meditation of the discursive kind, not so many teach the contemplative prayer that goes beyond thought and imagery into the supraconceptual cloud of unknowing. And it is precisely this that the English author (of the Cloud) is teaching. In his rejection of conceptualization, he is as radical as any Zen Buddhist. All thoughts, all concepts, all images must be buried beneath a cloud of forgetting, while our naked love [naked because divested of thought] must rise upward toward God hidden in the cloud of unknowing. With the cloud of unknowing above, between me and my God, and the cloud of forgetting below, between me and all creatures, I find myself in the *silentium mysticum* about which the English author read in the work of Dionysius."[20]

Many years ago a workman who came to my house to do some work spoke of the 'knowledge not found in books.' I was very surprised, but I never thought to ask him what he meant. It was only much later that I found the same words in Fr. Johnston's Introduction to the *Cloud of Unknowing*, and I often wondered was it possible that this is what the workman was referring to. In the Introduction, speaking again of Dionysius, Fr. Johnston writes as follows: "But there is yet a higher way of knowing God. 'Besides the knowledge of God obtained by processes of philosophical and theological speculation, there is that most divine knowledge of God which takes place through ignorance'; in this knowledge the intellect is illuminated by 'the unsearchable depth of wisdom.' Such knowledge is not found in books nor can it be obtained by human effort, for it is a divine gift. Man, however, can prepare himself to receive it; and this he does by prayer and purification."[21]

As I researched the meaning of contemplation and studied Father William Johnston's Introduction to the *Cloud of Unknowing*; and reread parts of the book, it seemed to me that mystical phenomena is not integral to contemplative prayer. But in reviewing my questions relative to the nature of mysticism, and considering what St. Teresa of Avila wrote, it certainly seems to be a debatable point! In my spiritual journey, it was not until I became acquainted with Father Thomas Keating's writings, that this issue, among others I have mentioned, was finally resolved to my satisfaction.

NINE

REVEALED TRUTHS

If mystical phenomena is not an integral part of mystical contemplation, what then is its purpose? Why do both St. John of the Cross and St. Teresa of Avila, devote many chapters to it? Or, in other words, why does God use such means to communicate with certain souls? It must be so that we can better understand Him with our limited and fallible human nature. The best examples that I can think of, relative to how God used mystical phenomena to communicate with us, can be found in studying how the revealed truths of the Catholic Church and the other Christian churches were established.

What is meant by revelation? The *Catechism of the Catholic Church* says that there is an order of knowledge, other than natural reason, by "which man cannot possibly arrive at by his own powers: the order of divine Revelation. Through an utterly free decision, God has revealed himself and given himself to man. This he does by revealing the mystery, his plan of loving goodness, formed from all eternity in Christ, for the benefit of all men. God has fully revealed this plan by sending us his beloved Son, our Lord Jesus Christ, and the Holy Spirit."[1] The Catechism states that the New Testament hands on the ultimate truth of God's revelation. Relative to the Old Testament is says that it "is an indispensable part of Sacred Scripture. Its books are divinely inspired and retain a permanent value, for the Old Covenant has never been revoked."[2] Thinking about these words, I decided to reexamine Sacred Scripture seeking to analyze the role mystical phenomena played in effecting these revealed truths.

A case in point, in the Old Testament, is the story of Abram, the father of the Jewish people. In Genesis, Chapter 12, Abram receives a divine locution as the Lord speaks to him saying: "Leave your own country, your kinsmen, and your father's house, and go to a country that I will show you. I will make you a great nation." (Gen. 11:1-2) It does not say that God appears to Abram, rather it says the God "speaks" to him. Abram, who is seventy-five years old, does the Lord's bidding, taking his wife, Sarai, and his nephew, Lot, with him. What was this locution like? How did Abram know that it was really God speaking to him? For a man his age it was quite an undertaking to leave his home and people, taking his family and his belongings because of some spiritual experience that he went through.

Much later in time, we learn that: "When Abraham was ninety-years old, the Lord appeared to him and said: 'I am God Almighty. Live always in my presence and be perfect, so that I may set my covenant between myself and you and multiply your descendants...I make this covenant, and I make it with you...Your name shall no longer be Abram, your name shall be Abraham, for I will make you father of a host of nations...I will fulfill my covenant between myself and you and your descendants after you, generation after generation, an everlasting covenant, to be your God, yours and your descendants after you.'" (Gen. 17:1-8) God also tells Abraham to change his wife's name from Sarai to Sarah and promises that he, Abraham, will have a son by Sarah. The delightful part of this story is how Abraham "throws himself on his face" and tries to hide his laughter because both he and his wife are far advanced in age. Notice that in this case, God not only speaks to Abraham, but He also "appears" to him. Compare it with St. Teresa's description quoted in the previous chapter. Later, Abraham and Sarah do have that son, Isaac, who becomes the next patriarch of the people.

Probably, the most famous story of the Old Testament deals with Moses and the Exodus of the Israelites out of

Egypt. The story of Moses is also replete with visions and locutions. We get an insight into Moses character as we read that Moses, seeing an Egyptian strike one of the Hebrew laborers, looks: "this way and that, and, seeing there was no one about, he struck the Egyptian down and hid his body in the sand." (Ex. 2:12-13) It is very revealing of his character at that point in time, and the question arises as to whether or not it can be considered murder. It is not unusual that God picks someone who is flawed as His representative. The Pharaoh tries to put Moses to death for his crime, but Moses escapes and flees to the land of Midian. Time passes, Moses marries, the Israelites remain in slavery in Egypt. Then one day, as Moses is tending his flock, he has his first recorded mystical experience, "an angel of the Lord appeared to him in the flame of a burning bush." God is within the burning bush and calls out to Moses: "I am the God of your forefathers, the God of Abraham, the God of Isaac, the God of Jacob." (Ex. 3:6)

Then God directs Moses to bring the Israelites out of slavery in Egypt. However, He predicts that the Pharaoh will not easily let them go, so God promises that He will work miracles so that the Israelites will be allowed to go. Moses responds that the Israelites themselves would never believe that the Lord had appeared to him. Then comes the part that seems more magical than mystical to me. The Lord gives Moses three signs to perform for the Israelites so that they may believe that Moses truly has been directed by God to bring them out of slavery in Egypt. For the first sign the Lord turns Moses' staff into a snake and then back again into a staff. Then He has Moses put his hand inside his cloak. When he withdraws it, his skin is leprous. Then He has Moses put it back inside his cloak and when he withdraws it the second time it has been returned to health. The Lord then says to Moses that if the people are not convinced by the first two miracles which Moses is to perform in front of them, that Moses should fetch some water from the Nile river, pour it on the ground and He would turn it into blood.

After convincing the Israelites with the three signs, Moses and his brother Aaron, who is to speak for Moses, approach the Pharaoh. As the Lord had predicted, Pharaoh refused to let the Israelites go. God then directs Moses to approach Pharaoh again, whose heart He had hardened. He explains to Moses that "I will make him stubborn. Then will I show sign after sign and portent after portent in the land of Egypt, and with mighty acts of judgment I will bring my people, the Israelites, out of Egypt…" (Ex. 7:3-4) Thereafter, Moses sequentially calls down ten plagues on the Egyptians, each time asking Pharaoh for permission to leave. And each time Pharaoh refuses.

For the first plague, Moses turns the Nile into blood. Scripture tells us that the Egyptian magicians did the same using their spells! For the second plague, Egypt is inundated with frogs and again the magicians do the same. However, when the third plague occurs wherein maggots infest the land, the plague cannot be duplicated by the Egyptian magicians. Finally, in the last and tenth plague, the Lord gives Moses instructions for celebrating the Lord's Passover. He tells Moses that the Israelites are to place the blood of a sacrificial lamb on the "two door-posts and on the lintel of every house in which they eat the lamb" and He continues: "On that night I shall pass through the land of Egypt and kill every first-born of man and beast. Thus will I execute judgement, I the Lord, against all the gods of Egypt. And as for you, the blood will be a sign on the houses in which you are; when I see the blood I will pass over you, the mortal blow shall not touch you, when I strike the land of Egypt." (Ex. 12:7,12-13) As soon as this plague occurs, Pharaoh relents and tells Moses that the Israelites may go.

How was I to interpret this story, particularly God visiting all these plagues on the Egyptians as well as the competition between the magicians and Moses? I found different explanations in various commentaries and Biblical footnotes. For example, one implied that the magicians made a snake rigid like a stick using hypnotism and other techniques and that no supernatural power was necessarily involved. A Biblical footnote regarding the ten plagues stressed that the literary purpose was to ridicule the deities. It suggested that the first plague was directed against the deified Nile and that the second plague against the frog-goddess, Heqet. The footnotes also suggested that, while there may be a natural explanation for the plagues, the story shows that in ending the plagues, the God of Israel controls nature. In Lawrence Boadt's book, *Reading the Old Testament,* published by the Paulist Press, he makes similar claims. He says that: "The first nine plagues all have a natural explanation in conditions found even today in Egypt."[3] However, he also stresses that the Israelites recognized as miraculous God's control in ending these plagues.

What is a sticking point for me is the idea that God would visit death on all the Egyptian first-born children. The only reference I found among my books about the tenth plague was Lawrence Boadt's book in which he writes: "The tenth and final plague stands apart. Although it may seem coldly brutal to us, Israel saw the death of Egypt's first-born as God's clear choice on behalf of his people and his life-and-death concern for their freedom."[4] God's taking the lives of the "first-born of man and beast" is a hard mystery for me to accept. The answer may lie in God's words quoted earlier: "I will execute judgment against all the gods of Egypt." This incident in the Old Testament is one of a number of questionable acts alleged to have been wrought by God. It is not all that easy to read certain parts of the Old Testament because of this. I find it hard to believe that God "causes" any evil in this world. I realize that the question of whether or not God causes evil, is a very difficult one and I leave it to the theologians to resolve. However, despite what may seem as a contradiction in terms, I would rather believe that God "allows," but does not "cause" these things, like murder, sickness or natural calamities to occur.

Relative to this idea of God allowing rather than directly causing these tragedies, I have profited greatly from reading the writings of Vassula Ryden, the Greek Orthodox mystic. In particular, she has helped me to better understand and appreciate the Old Testament scriptures. What some may consider a novel idea addressed in the messages is that we, rather than God, are the source of so many of the problems facing mankind today. All of us can surely think of many ways that our actions have been destructive to the planet. For example, the serious impact of DDT in our environment which was made clear to many of us in reading Rachel Carson's book, *Silent Spring*. Visible to the naked eye is the pollution in so many of our lakes, rivers and streams. And, of course, there is the extinction of so very many forms of life in the animal kingdom. I'm sure that the reader can list even more serious problems.

There are a number of examples in Vassula's messages in which God refers to our guilt in events such as we have just referred to in the previous paragraph, and yet in a positive tone He expresses how important it is for us to become children of His Light. This is what Jesus said to Vassula in August 1988: "be just to each other and kind to each other, <u>love one another,</u> become children of My Light; understand how so many catastrophes are drawn upon you, they are drawn by the evil that has accumulated in your soul;" (True Life In God {TLIG} 8-15-1988) Much later, in February 2002 God makes specific reference to the United States and what happened on 9/11. "Considering therefore, your reluctance to a true metanoia, and how you have shown hostility instead towards My Warnings, what former scenes of wailing took place (9/11) are nothing in comparison to the sorrowful mornings that lie ahead of you; sorrowful mornings that will be drawn by your own hand;" (TLIG 2-7-2002) Further on in the same message God directly addresses our original question: 'Who causes natural calamities not only now but also in the Old Testament?' With sorrow, God tells us that: "today, with grief, I see from above how your designs will turn against yourselves; the world already is tasting the fruits of its own course, provoking nature to rebel with convulsions, drawing upon yourselves natural catastrophes," (TLIG 2-7-2002) If this happens in New Testament times I wonder if it also was operative in the calamities cited in the Old Testament history.

In the New Testament two particular mystical incidents stand out in my mind. The first is the transfiguration when Jesus took Peter, James and John the brother of James to the top of a high mountain. There Jesus was "transfigured; his face shone like the sun, and his clothes became white as the light. And they saw Moses and Elijah appear, conversing with him." Then, while Peter was speaking to Jesus, "a bright cloud suddenly overshadowed them, and a voice called from the cloud: 'This is my beloved Son'" (Matt. 17:2-6) Notice that in this incident no one sees God the Father. He is hidden within the cloud and only His voice can be heard. Notice also the reference to Elijah, the mystery man of the Old Testament, who was taken up to heaven while he is still alive, as his disciple, Elisha, watches. More about Elijah and the Second Coming later.

The second mystical occurrence that stands out in my mind is the conversion of Saul of Tarsus on the road to Damascus. As I reread Chapter nine of the *Acts of the Apostles*, I am struck by the strong language used to depict Saul's demeanor. The first sentence reads: "meanwhile Saul was still breathing murderous threats against the disciples of the Lord." (Acts 9:1) More than once in this chapter there are words depicting how the disciples were afraid of Saul and did not trust his conversion. Yet it was this man that the Lord picked to become the Apostle to the Gentiles.

Most of us know the story of how a light comes from heaven and surrounds Saul as he travels the road to Damascus. Saul and his companions then hear a voice saying: "Saul, Saul why do you persecute Me?" And in response to Saul's question as to who he was, the voice answered: "I am Jesus, whom you are persecuting." (Acts 9:4-6) Then Jesus tells Saul to go to Damascus and await instructions. When Saul opens his eyes he discovers that he is blind. Thereafter, in Damascus Saul has a vision of Ananias and is told that Ananias will lay hands on him and Saul will recover his sight. Saul, of course, becomes St. Paul who brings Christianity to the gentiles, the author of a number of epistles in the New Testament and a martyr for the faith.

I had always assumed that at the time of Paul's conversion that he learned about Christ and His teachings through the other Apostles. However, Paul makes a very telling and dramatic statement in his Letter to the Galatians where he claims: "I must make it clear to you, my friends, that the gospel you heard me preach is no human invention. I did not take it over from any man; no man taught it me; I received it through a revelation of Jesus Christ." (Gal. 1:11-12)

These are two of the most dramatic stories in the New Testament and they demonstrate how, like the Old Testament, God uses mystical means of communicating His Revelation to us. As I quoted earlier, the Catholic Catechism stresses that the Bible is the main source of Revelation, of the revealed truths held by the Catholic Church. To thus accept the Bible as the main source of Divine Revelation is to also accept the fact that visions and locutions do indeed happen, and that God is the source of some of them. It also points out that one of the major reasons that God seems to use these mystical phenomena is to be able to reach out and teach us about Himself on our level.

TEN

RATIONALISM

Over the years, my spiritual journey has been impacted by the culture of which I am a part, not only the secular culture but also the religious culture. After Vatican II, I felt somewhat adrift and confused. There seemed to be so many new and different interpretations of Catholic positions. Consequently, I subjected more things religious to critical evaluation.

In reading a friend's blog on the internet, I learned that he did not believe in God. He implied that evolution and reason proved that God did not exist. This is a bright young man with a college education. At about the same time, I came upon an article in the Philadelphia Inquirer newspaper dated Sept.10, 2006, titled: Believer or not, we can Coexist, by Jennifer Michael Hecht. She is an atheist, historian, poet and teacher at the New School University, and an author. She points out that: "Throughout history, atheists have felt little need to spread their ideas. Why bother? Everyone knew the university was the place to find secular thought, so there wasn't much need to advertise. And for 2,500 years, most nonbelievers were not furious at religion. They thought the masses needed it or wanted it and they did not think that would ever change, so they set themselves to living in peace with it. In fact, the sages told their students to participate in local religion, and enjoy the sweet and simple metaphysics."

However, in recent times the atheists are being provoked by the fact that an allegedly religious group has gained political power here in the United States. For example,

Jennifer Hecht claims that the decision to go to war in Iraq was a decision based on prayer. Another example she gives is that "Our president smiles and pushes the test tubes into the garbage." Her argument is basically that religion is playing a more active role in our government and that the atheists won't stand by and let this happen. Jennifer Hecht goes on to say: "Lately, however, a lot of atheists have begun calling for a complete rejection of religion. These are extraordinary, already-famous people who could easily be writing about other topics but have decided to write about this one." She claims that these prominent atheists have temporarily turned from their fields of work and are now making a point of haranguing us instead. She claims they are doing this because "they have been provoked." This new, militant stance is a concern to me.

At the same time there appeared in Newsweek magazine an article dated Sept.11, 2006, titled The New Naysayers, by Jerry Adler in which he points out that we are in the midst of a religious revival in America. Adler bases his claim on the results of a recent Newsweek Poll in which "Americans said they believed in God by a margin of 92 to 6 – only two percent answered 'don't know.'" He stresses the fact that despite this alleged religious revival, three atheists, Richard Dawkins, Sam Harris and Daniel C. Dennett, have all just written books opposing religion with "bone-rattling attacks on what they regard as a pernicious outdated superstition." He concludes his article with the following prediction: "If Dawkins, Dennett and Harris are right, the five-century-long competition between science and religion is sharpening. People are choosing sides. And when that happens, people get hurt."

Although my Chapter 11, titled Physicists and Mystics, does not directly address this conflict between science and religion, I do point out that Ken Wilber, American author, practicing Buddhist and founder of the Integral Institute has a different point of view. He does not believe that there is any conflict between the Science of Physics and religion! On the other hand, he does not believe that physics supports a mystical view of the world at all, or a religious view!

What has all this to do with the impact of both the secular and religious culture on me and my spiritual journey? In answering that question I feel that a number of points have to be made first. Although the atheists may be small in number, their ideas can have major impacts on how we perceive things and on how we believe. My catholic dictionary defines rationalism as follows: "A system of thought or attitude of mind which holds that human reason is self-sufficient and does not need the help of divine revelation to know all that is necessary for a person's well being. Also the view that a priori reason can give certitude without experience or verification of facts."[1] A 1911 Catholic Encyclopedia I found on the internet indicates that rationalistic systems are many and atheism is just one of them. It further claims that the rationalistic tendency "has always existed in philosophy, and has generally shown itself powerful in all the critical schools."[2]

One of the reasons that I became interested in rationalism was the example I cited above about the young friend of mine who wrote on his blog that reason and evolution disproved the existence of God. Another, more powerful reason that I wanted to learn about rationalism and atheism, which is a form of rationalism, is the fact that Vassula Ryden, the Greek Orthodox mystic and visionary, has numerous references to rationalism in the divinely inspired messages which she has been receiving from God, beginning in Bangladesh on September 20, 1986 to the present day. For more information on Vassula see Chapter 14 and Chapter 15.

Relative to rationalism, here is a message from God which Vassula received in 1988 in which He tells us that we are living in the End of Times. He tells us that He had warned us of these times and that "it has also been said that in your times only a remnant of My servants would remain faithful to Me, preaching the Gospel as it should be preached, and that many would fall into rationalism, betraying Me with disloyalty, this rationalism made a desert of My Church, bringing It into a ruin where vipers nestled within Its depths;" (TLIG 9-27-88) Almost three years later, God gives a message to Vassula which shows His tender concern: "I have counted My sheep and My Heart is crushed with sorrow, only a remnant are left today who have not been raided by Apostasy; only a handful have not lost their faith; only a few are left who survived the perils of Rationalism," (TLIG 5-6-91) Further on in this same message God explains how He plans to revive us, to save us. He states: "Apostasy challenged My Mercy and Rationalism, this plague of your era, challenged My Power; I am sending before Me, to educate you, the Woman clothed with the Sun, the second Eve, to school you and lead you step by step into Heaven;" (TLIG 5-6-91)

Because of this emphasis on rationalism in Vassula's messages; and reading about Richard Dawkins' book, *The God Delusion,* in the Newsweek article I quoted above; and recognizing my lack of knowledge as to where the atheists were coming from in their ideas on religion and science; I decided to order the Dawkins' book from Amazon. I hoped this would help me better understand how rationalistic atheists viewed the roles of reason and science in our modern era. When I was a teenager I had questioned whether or not the Catholic Church was, as it claimed, the true Church of Christ. I used to read the lives of converts to Catholicism in order to learn what convinced them. As an adult, I have struggled with the question, a number of times, as to whether or not God really exists. However, I had never before read a book by an atheist as to why he did not believe in God and why we shouldn't.

Since 1995, Richard Dawkins has been the Charles Simonyi Professor of the Public Understanding of Science at

Oxford University. He has written at least six other books. The blurb on the jacket of his book reads as follows: "A preeminent scientist – and the world's most prominent atheist – asserts the irrationality of belief in God and the grievous harm religion has inflicted on society from the Crusades to 9/11."

I have read and marked points, which seemed key to my understanding of his positions, in the first 159 pages of the book, and glanced through the rest of its 215 pages of text. He is universal in his condemnation of all religions. This is what he has to say about belief in God: "The God Hypothesis suggests that the reality we inhabit also contains a supernatural agent who designed the universe and – at least in many versions of the hypothesis – maintains it and even intervenes in it with miracles, which are temporary violations of his own otherwise grandly immutable laws."[4] In talking about the problems of evolution versus creationism, he quotes his colleague the Chicago geneticist Jerry Coyne, who writes about Dawkins' position on this topic as follows: "To scientists like Dawkins and Wilson [E. O. Wilson, the celebrated Harvard biologist], the *real* war is between rationalism and superstition. Creationism is just a symptom of what they see as the greater enemy: religion."[5]

In Dawkins' fourth chapter titled: "Why There Almost Certainly Is No God" (He explains the heading based on the fact that he believes that there is only a very small likelihood that God exists.), he summarizes the position of the Creationists as follows: "Creationist 'logic' is always the same. Some natural phenomenon is too statistically improbable, too complex, too beautiful, too awe inspiring to have come into existence by chance. Design is the only alternative to chance that the authors can imagine. Therefore a designer must have done it. And science's answer to this faulty logic is also the same. Design is not the only alternative to chance. Natural selection is a better alternative. Indeed, design is not a real alternative at all because it raises an even bigger problem than it solves: who designed the designer? Chance and design both fail as solutions to the problem of statistical improbability, because one of them is the problem, and the other regresses to it. Natural selection is a real solution. It is the only workable solution, it is a solution of stunning elegance and power."[6]

I have struggled with this question of who created the designer a number of times and my answer is always the same. I ask myself: "What is more difficult to believe, that the universe came out of nothing, or that God came out of nothing?" To put it grossly, I find it easier to believe that God came out of nothing than to believe that the universe came out of nothing. Or to put it more elegantly, God did not require a creator because, by definition, by His very nature, He does not require a creator. The belief that a creator of God is required is based on man's limited knowledge and reasoning power. Although finite man can define God in terms of what God is not, and although he can express the concept of infinity mathematically, he cannot comprehend an infinite God!

In his penultimate chapter titled: Childhood, Abuse and Religion, Dawkins says that the main purpose of the chapter is to consider the following question: "isn't it always a form of child abuse to label children as possessors of beliefs that they are too young to have thought about?"[7] Later, he adds: "Our Society, including the non-religious sector, has accepted the preposterous idea that it is normal and right to indoctrinate tiny children in the religion of their parents, and to slap religious labels on them, 'Catholic child,' 'Protestant child,' 'Jewish child,' 'Muslim child,' etc."[8] We, in America, live in a free society and parents can teach their children as they think best. My personal opinion is that it would be cruel indeed to deny the child the belief in a loving God, who seeks their love in return; and is always caring for them; and who asks that they love others as God loves them.

Why does God place so much emphasis on rationalism in His messages to Vassula? As I have noted above, atheism is a form of rationalism. Both Richard Dawkins and Jennifer Hecht refer to the universities as a sort of haven for atheism. Those ideas and theories which are commonly accepted in the universities, but not as much by the general public, tend to trickle down and slowly modify our beliefs without our realizing what is happening.

These trickle down theories come to us via books, lectures and from the university students themselves. For example, religion cited as the most common form of superstition, resides in my subconscious and I sense it from time to time when I think of others and what they think of religion. The idea that it is wrong to teach religion to little children has been accepted by many intellectuals. They frequently say: "I don't believe that religion should be taught to a child who is so easily influenced by its parents. Rather, let them decide about religion when they grow up." From time to time I hear or read about Mary, the Mother of God, being a goddess, as if the honor we pay to her were some sort of pagan worship. And in Catholic circles I sense an uneasiness about professing belief in miracles and often hear that such and such happening could easily be explained by natural causes. Where did most such ideas originate or spread, powerfully affecting so many of us, if not from the universities?

One strong reaction that I exhibited, and I blame it on the rationalism that has permeated our society and unconsciously influenced me, was how uncomfortable I was, at first, in talking about the two visionaries, Gianna Sullivan and Vassula Ryden. I did not want to admit that I believed that their messages came from God. I could just imagine my peers thinking: "In this day and age, how could anyone with any intelligence, be taken in by such superstitous nonsense?" This is documented in a letter I wrote to Father Thomas Keating on Jan. 19, 2002. In the letter I tell him about the two visionaries and about my plans for my web site, JesusofMercy.com. Then I write: "I have to admit that there are times when I think that when I turn on my web site I will be subject to ridicule because of my belief in these apparitions and messages. Then I ask myself how could I possibly worry about something like that at my age! But I do."

One definition of rationalism implies that reason is the sole source and final test of all truth. Obviously I don't believe that. But I do believe in the importance of reason. I can recall one day as I was facilitating a Bible study group in my home, I said something, I don't remember exactly what, but it was to the effect that reason was very important in religion. To a person, they all laughed at me! I didn't pursue the topic any further, but it did upset me. I never knew whether I expressed myself poorly or what.

Pope Benedict XVI was making that very point about reason in his recent address in Regensburg, Batavia. It was the address that aroused so much controversy about the Muslim religion and its alleged ties to violence. In an article in the Sept. 25, 2006 Newsweek magazine titled The Pope's 'Holy War' Jon Meacham points out that:

> "Much of the Regensburg address was a meditation on faith and reason, the roots of religiously inspired violence and the need for believers to see God as a figure of Love. Roughly put, his argument was this: to Benedict, Islam's conception of God so stresses God's will that God can be understood to command the irrational. For the pope, the Christian encounter with the classical world married faith and reason and thereby precluded, in principle, such misunderstandings of the nature of the God of Abraham, a nature that is, according to this argument, rooted in love and reason, not the will to dominance. Seen in such a light, 'jihad,' which

> means 'struggle,' can too easily be taken literally [as a call to violence against others] rather than figuratively [as many Muslim scholars argue it should be.]
>
> "In the stormy aftermath of the address – on Saturday two churches in the West Bank were bombed – the Vatican argued that the real point of the lecture was to be found in this sentence: 'A reason which is deaf to the divine and which relegates religion into the realm of subcultures,' Benedict said 'is incapable of entering into the dialogue of cultures.'"

The article goes on to quote George Weigel, Catholic theologian and papal biographer, who describes Pope Benedict XVI as having "'a hardheaded conversation' about the role of faith in the life of the world. 'He knew exactly what he was doing' says Weigel. 'He is saying that irrational violence is displeasing to God.' The question Benedict is putting on the table is 'Does a significant part of Islam have the capacity to be self-critical?'"

In an article in the Philadelphia Inquirer newspaper of Sept. 24, 2006, Christopher Levenick, a W. H. Brady Fellow at the American Enterprise Institute, under the heading Reason and Faith Enrich Each Other, had this to say: "At Regensburg, Benedict challenged modern Europe to consider the proper use of reason. The implications of his argument are profound. Benedict believes that reason, rightly understood, lies at the very heart of Western civilization – and its corruption represents a grave threat to civilization."

According to Christopher Levenick, Pope Benedict stresses the fundamental need to address the nature of reason itself. While the Pope acknowledges the importance and benefits to mankind of the scientific method, Christopher Levenick writes that: "But though science is good, it is not the only good. Science admits its own limits, and reason points to possibilities outside of reason. Western civilization, Benedict concludes, can gain from Christian theology the '**courage to engage the whole breadth of reason.**'" (emphasis mine)

ELEVEN

PHYSICISTS AND MYSTICS

When I graduated with a Bachelor of Science degree cum laude from the City College of New York with a major in Physics, I ranked second in my graduating class. Despite this high ranking, if anyone asked me about my education I was quick to gloss over the fact that physics was my major, and I changed the subject as soon as possible. The reason I did this was because I never felt I really understood physics!

Soon after I retired, my husband bought a book that had been recently published, *Mathematics and the Search for Knowledge* by Morris Kline. As I glanced at the index I noted that Kline was addressing many of the topics in physics that had left me puzzled, such as Maxwell's Law, Relativity and Quantum Mechanics. Since I had much more time at my disposal now that I was retired, I started to read it carefully and slowly, hoping it would give me a better understanding of physics. Ironically, I always thought that my husband, who had an undergraduate degree in Engineering from Penn State and a Master's degree in Mathematics from New York University, knew more about physics than I did! As you read this chapter on Physicists and Mystics, I think that you will see why I came to realize that this was indeed true, due to his mathematical background and his approach to abstract concepts.

Morris Kline was a Professor of Mathematics, Emeritus, at New York University and consequently he stressed in his book, *Mathematics and the Search for Knowledge*, the mathematical aspects of physics. In his Preface he points out:

"Contrary to the impression students acquire in school, mathematics is not just a series of techniques. Mathematics tells us what we have never known or even suspected about notable phenomena and in some instances even contradicts perception. It is the essence of our knowledge of the physical world. It not only transcends perception but outclasses it."[1] Later he explains: "We must go beyond perceptual knowledge. The essence of mathematics, as opposed to sense perceptions, is that it draws on the human mind and human reasoning to produce knowledge about our physical world that the average human being, even in Western culture, believes is acquired by the use of sense perceptions."[2]

The history of the scientific theories of the universe provide interesting examples of the impact of sense perceptions in the development of those theories. Some time after the year 300 BC a Greek astronomer, Aristarchus of Samos proposed a scientific heliocentric model of the solar system with the sun, not the earth, as the center of the universe. However, it was mostly speculative. Approximately five hundred years later, in 200 AD, Ptolemy proposes a geocentric theory in which the *earth was the center of the universe* and the sun and planets revolved around it. From approximately 1500 onwards several astronomers began to propose once again, a heliocentric theory of the universe. Copernicus was one of these astronomers. Then, Galileo in his book published in 1632, *Dialogue on the Great World Systems* presented his heliocentric theory of the universe in which the *sun was the center of the universe* rather than the then accepted geocentric theory. In 1633 his book was put on the Index of Prohibited Books of the Catholic Church and this ban was not lifted until 1822. The trial of Galileo is often cited as the beginning of the conflict between science and religion.

In the year 1900, the astronomer Bessel succeeded in measuring the distance to the nearest star beyond the sun. It turned out to be approximately 25 *million, million* miles away as compared to the sun's distance from the earth which is considered just 93 *million* miles away. These findings proved beyond a doubt that neither the earth nor the sun was the *center of the universe.* Morris Kline points out in his book, *Mathematics and the Search for Knowledge,* that: "The same observational data that Hipparchus and Ptolemy organized in their geocentric theory of deferent and epicycle can also be organized under the heliocentric theory of Copernicus and Kepler. Despite the belief of the latter that the new theory was true, the modern view is that either theory will do and there is no need to adopt the heliocentric hypothesis except to gain mathematical simplicity."[3] Despite this modern view, it should be realized that Galileo made impressive contributions to science. As Morris Kline points out: "With the *Discourses* of 1638 Galileo launched modern physical science on its mathematical course, founded the modern science of mechanics, and set the pattern for all of modern scientific thought."[4]

In talking about Newton's universal law of gravitation, Morris Kline makes a very surprising statement. He says: "Contrary to popular belief, no one has ever explained the physical reality of the force of gravitation. It is a fiction suggested by the human ability to exert force. **The greatest science fiction stories are in the science of Physics.** However, mathematical deductions from the quantitative law proved so effective that this procedure has been accepted as an integral part of physical science. What science has done, then, is to sacrifice physical intelligibility for the sake of mathematical description and mathematical prediction."[5] (emphasis mine) He expands on this idea further by pointing out that: "In Newton's time and for two hundred years afterwards, physicists spoke of the action of gravity as 'action at a distance,' a meaningless phrase that was accepted as a substitute for explaining the physical mechanism, much as we speak of spirits or ghosts to explain unseen phenomena."[6] I think that they were still using the phrase 'action at a distance' in the 20th century when I was going to school. It was one of those expressions in physics whose meaning escaped me.

In writing about Maxwell's laws, Morris Kline states that: "Just as Newton's laws of motion furnished scientists with the means for working with matter and force without explaining either, so Maxwell's equations have enabled scientists to accomplish wonders with electrical phenomena despite a woefully deficient understanding of their physical nature…Elcctrons, electric and magnetic fields, and ether waves merely provide names for the variables that appear in the formulas or, as von Helmholtz stated the point, in Maxwell's theory an electric charge is but the recipient of a symbol."[7]!!!

Morris Kline's book provides not only a history of physics but also a history of the impact of physical theories on philosophy and on religious concepts. In talking about the mechanistic view of the universe he states: "in the light of more recent developments, mechanism or materialism is not tenable. Ether as a substance has been abandoned, and only mathematical laws replace it. Gravitational force has been replaced by relativistic geodesics in space-time. We accept the propagation of electromagnetic waves whose physical nature is unknown. We are also asked to accept a particle-wave duality that defies common sense, as if, by magic, electrons that are particles become waves when ejected from atoms. Relativity and quantum mechanics especially call for a profound revision of classical mechanics."[8]

Although many of the answers I was looking for were actually implied in the quotes above, I did not recognize them! After reading the book almost two times, the major concept that I came away with was the important role of mathematics in modern physics. Morris Kline's book left me with a sense of awe and a new respect for what Mathematics had made possible and how man came to recognize and employ this power.

At that point in my retirement, I put the questions of physics out of my mind. I had had enough of science and technology! I spent many years going to graduate school at night and also working long hours as an Engineering Research Section Head. I wanted to do other things now that I was retired. And I did! I took courses in painting with acrylics and watercolors. I facilitated a Little Rock Bible study group and a Centering Prayer group in Notre Dame parish until we moved from Long Island. I learned to play bridge, something I wanted to do since I was a teenager. I spent time gardening and investing in real estate.

My husband worked so hard and traveled so much when he was employed, that we had shared very little time together in those years. I looked at retirement as an opportunity to spend much more time doing things together. I was not disappointed! While we have many separate interests, we have found that retirement affords us much more time together and we make every use of it.

I also attended a series of lectures on contemplative prayer given by the late Rev. John B. Healey S.T.L. He was a member of the Brooklyn Diocese. He was a teacher and also wrote a column for the Brooklyn Tablet newspaper. I was delighted when I heard of his lectures since, as I have mentioned before, mystical contemplation was hardly, if ever, referenced in my environment. In an article he wrote for America magazine, dated Feb. 19, 1994, titled The Journey Within, he talks about his spiritual journey. He writes: "I am 82 years of age, and have been an ordained priest for 57 of those years. One would ordinarily expect that a priest who has been active in the ministry of the church for so long a time would, by the very nature of that experience, be truly knowledgeable and practiced in the ways of Christian prayer. Not so with me."!!! Fr. Healey points out that during the course of his life he had said countless prayers, yet: "it is only now, in the twilight of my days, that I am finally learning how to pray and, by God's grace, becoming a prayerful person."

Fr. Healey wrote that when he was ordained he: "was top-heavy with doctrine. I knew about God, but I did not know God." He adds that around 1984 the writings of Thomas Merton "began to provoke my interest in contemplation. I spent more and more time in silent, wordless prayer. Two intense retreats under the direction of Abbott Thomas Keating, a Trappist, made me realize that at last I had found the way to pray that my heart had always longed for, though I knew it not." In the writings of those modern visionaries who impressed me so very much, God keeps asking us to pray with our hearts. In his humility, Fr. Healey admits that, although he was a priest for more than 55 years, he had not known how to really pray, to pray with his heart, until he was in his seventies. From that time on, his one goal seemed to be to teach Centering Prayer to everyone!

I also took courses on Christian mystics given by Father John Garkowski, of the Diocese of Brooklyn, at the Immaculate Conception Center in Douglaston, NY. He was a parish priest with a law degree and he spent much of his spare time helping immigrants, for free, with their legal problems. He was also an avid traveler. But what impressed me most was his extraordinary enthusiasm for the study of the great Christian mystics.

I attended a number of his courses given on different mystics, some of whom included Julian of Norwich, Teresa of Avila, Catherine of Siena and Meister Eckhart. He would have handouts of excerpts from the writings of these mystics with his own markings on them. He had an uncanny way of picking out the key religious positions in each of their writings.

During that period of time I gave no further thought to my questions relative to the nature of physics. However, a short time ago, my sister the nun, told me that she planned to take a one-week course sponsored by Retreats International at Loyola University in Chicago. The subject of the course and the associated text book was *Quantum Theology*. I immediately expressed an interest. After the course she sent me the book on *Quantum Theology*, as well as a second book, titled *Quantum Questions*, edited by Ken Wilber. I glanced through the first book, but not being particularly impressed by it, sent it back to my sister. I started to read the second book, *Quantum Questions*, and found it absolutely fascinating. I could not put it down. Right away, I started to mark it up, as I do with most books that I find very interesting, and in which I want to highlight points that seem key to me, for further reference. Consequently, I had to quickly order another book from Amazon so that my sister would still have her own unmarked copy.

Quantum Questions contains the mystical writings of the world's greatest physicists, including Heisenberg, Schroedinger, Einstein, De Broglie, Jeans, Planck, Pauli and Eddington. It is edited by Ken Wilber, who is an American writer and practicing Buddhist. He is considered the most influential integral theorist today and is founder of the Integral Institute. Integral Theory is a relatively new and developing movement by philosophers and teachers who seek a comprehensive understanding of humans and the universe. In his Preface to the 2001 edition of his book, Ken Wilber writes that because of the increasing interest of the modern world in topics relating to science and religion, he feels that it is wise to revisit the writings of the men who were pioneers in the creation of modern physics. With this intention in mind, he makes the point that: "*Quantum Questions* is a compendium of virtually all of the significant writings from some of the greatest physicists the world has ever known."[9]

He goes on to discuss how many people today, particularly in the New Age category, believe that modern physics supports a mystical world view. Contrary to this view, Ken Wilber clearly reiterates the point that, in fact, physics does not support a mystical view of the world at all, or a religious view! He expounds on this further by stating that these eight physicists whose writings are published in his book: "simply believed, to a man, that if modern physics no longer objects to a religious world view, it offers no positive support either; properly speaking, it is indifferent to all that"[10] However, he adds an interesting statement, which is the basis for his book. Talking of the physicists whose writings are included in Quantum Questions, he says: "They rejected the notion that physics proves or even supports mysticism, and *yet every one of them was an avowed mystic!*"[11]

The question arises as to: "What does Ken Wilber mean by mysticism?" He may have defined mysticism in his book, but I didn't find it. However, it seems to me that he leaves it up to the reader, as he evaluates the writings of the eight physicists included in *Quantum Questions*, to determine for himself what sort of mystic each physicist was. For my purposes, I would like to use two different definitions. I would like to make a distinction between natural mystical experience, which may relate to some of these eight physicists, and supernatural mystical experience. I equate natural mysticism to one or more experiences, which the majority of people have at one time or another, in which they somehow feel that they are one with the object of their contemplation. (A personal God is not required in this definition.) Such experiences could be triggered by the joy and awe we might feel as we watch an unusually beautiful sunset over the ocean; or the love and happiness we might experience as we simply go for a walk with the one we love above all others; or the many joy filled intellectual experiences when something mentally challenging suddenly falls into place.

Heisenberg discusses this sort of intellectual experience in a chapter on Science and the Beautiful, in Ken Wilber's book, where he questions how that which is beautiful relates to exact science. He describes how he was reading the work of the mathematician Leopold Kronecker when he "sensed a quite immediate beauty in the fact that, from the problem of partitioning a circle, whose simplest cases were, of course, familiar to us in school, it was possible to learn something about the totally different sort of questions involved in elementary number theory."[12]

He goes on to point out how the recognition of this abstract beauty plays a role when advances in exact science such as relativity or quantum theory are made. He writes: "in both cases, after years of vain effort at understanding, a bewildering plethora of details has been almost suddenly reduced to order by the appearance of a connection, largely unintuitable, but still ultimately simple in its substance, that was immediately found convincing by virtue of its completeness and abstract beauty – convincing, that is, to all who could understand and speak such an abstract language."[13]

Relative to supernatural mysticism, there are different forms, but I am generally speaking of Christian mysticism unless otherwise noted. Also, when I talk about my aspirations to mystical contemplation, I most frequently think in terms of being united to the Trinity as the ultimate goal of a disciplined, wordless prayer in which my soul seeks (or yearns for, or burns with love for) the Godhead through the *cloud of unknowing*. In my daily periods of meditation (Eastern definition, not discursive) I try to rest in God, silently aware of and consenting to His presence and action in my soul. This is beautifully explained in Father Thomas Keating's' book, *Open Mind, Open Heart*.

My reading of the book, *Quantum Questions*, became for me a natural mystical experience of the intellectual kind, in which I was filled with a feeling of awe and wonder relative to how Ken Wilber, although it was not the prime intent of his book, answered the questions about physics that had bothered me since I was an undergraduate in the City College of New York. It was truly an epiphany for me!!! It all came together when I suddenly realized, to my amazement, that the reason I had so much trouble understanding physics was that **physics,**

in actual fact, wasn't understandable! Clearly this needs to be explained.

What do I mean by the words: "physics, in actual fact, wasn't understandable?" For all my life prior to retirement, I was puzzled as to how scientists got their knowledge of the universe. I wondered where all their physical laws originated. That's why, when I retired, I decided to carefully read and study Morris Kline's book, *Mathematics and the Search for Knowledge*. I felt that I had both the education and background to help me find these answers. However, after a thorough reading of Morris Kline's book, I was a bit overwhelmed by the breadth and depth of what he had written; and, as I indicated earlier, I decided to drop the subject and take up other interests.

Apparently, Morris Kline's book had planted a lot of ideas in my subconscious. After reading Ken Wilber's book, *Quantum Questions*, all of these ideas suddenly came together and Morris Kline's book took on new meaning! It became clear to me that Morris Kline's book contained the ideas and statements necessary to support the principal points that Ken Wilber was making about physics. However, these ideas were competing with a substantial amount of historical data and mathematical issues that Morris Kline was also addressing in his book. Consequently, I hadn't been able to put all the pertinent statements into one coherent whole, relative to the nature of the reality that these modern laws of physics conjured up.

One of the first points I quoted, at the beginning of this chapter from *Mathematics and the Search for Knowledge*, was that mathematics played a bigger role in physics than many of us understood. Morris Kline explains that mathematics tells us things about the world around us that, in the past, were never suspected. Moreover, many of these things about the physical world, that the average person believes are based on human sense perceptions, in actual fact, are not. I, too, believed that physical observation based on the use of the senses was the very essence of the Scientific Method. But what Morris Kline says is that, not only are these physical laws not based solely on sense perceptions, but in some cases they are actually contradictory!

Most of us can think of an example of an apparent contradiction, such as: "If the earth is round, why don't we fall off it?" This certainly contradicts our sense perceptions; but we immediately answer: "We don't fall off because of the Law of Gravity, that is, the gravitational pull of the earth keeps us from falling into space." But as I quoted above, Morris Kline wrote: "no one has ever explained the physical reality of the force of gravitation. It is a **fiction** suggested by the human ability to exert force." (emphasis mine)[5]

Kline also points out that gravity is a quantitative law from which the mathematical deductions were so convincing that it has become an accepted physical law, even though it means that science has sacrificed "physical intelligibility for the sake of mathematical description and mathematical prediction."[5] Newton was very clear about this point in his book, *Principia.* He writes: "For I have design only to give a mathematical notion of the forces, without considering their physical causes and seats."[14] Because of this, Newton considered his work incomplete. He even wrote to a friend some very surprising words which give us a better insight into his thinking at that time. He writes: "That one body may act upon another at a distance through a vacuum without the mediation of anything else, by and through which their action and force may be conveyed from one to another, is to me so great an *absurdity* that, I believe, no man who has in philosophic matters a competent faculty of thinking could ever fall into it."[15] (italics mine)

It is easy to be deceived by these deprecating words of Newton regarding his Law of Gravity and to thereby think that it must not be all that useful to physics. However, before

Newton's work, it was generally thought that the fields of terrestrial science and of celestial science were not related to each other. Newton proved otherwise with his Law of Gravity. While his contributions to science were many, what interests me most is the fact that his emphasis on the use of mathematics in describing physical phenomena is the key to the amazing developments in modern physics. It is also the key to Morris Kline's statement relative to the "greatest science fiction stories"[5] being in the fields of physics.

Part of my confusion about science, was the fact that I thought when the scientific method was invoked, it involved being able to repeatedly perform some experiment which could be observed and verified by others. And I didn't see how gravity fit into that definition. Newton himself pointed out that the "motions of the planets, the comets, the moon and the sea"[16] are deduced mathematically from his original equations of gravity. In other words, my problem was created by the definition of the scientific method I was trying to employ. In his book, *Quantum Questions*, Ken Wilber goes into the definition of the scientific method when he begins to address the relationship between science and religion. He points out that frequently, the apparent conflicts between science and religion are caused by the way we define science and how we differentiate between the "*domain* of science" and the "*method* of science."[17]

It is not my intention to address the issue of science versus religion. I want to write about the scientific method and the difficulty I had in applying it. However, with regard to our use of domains, I would like to mention that Ken Wilber goes into the subject of science versus religion when he applies the so-called "Great Chain of Being" to five domains: spirit, soul, mind, life and matter. It is an excellent exposition of how these domains relate to each other and to representative disciplines that take these domains as an object of study.

What was of great help to me were the following statements and his related explanations of their importance: "On the one hand, then, spirit is the *highest* of all possible domains; it is the Summit of all realms, the Being beyond all beings. It is the domain that is a subset of no other domain, and thus preserves its radically transcendental nature. On the other hand, since spirit is all-pervading and all-inclusive, since it is the set of all possible sets, the Condition of all conditions and Nature of all natures, it is not properly thought of as a realm set apart from other realms, but as the Ground or Being of *all* realms, the pure *That* of which all manifestation is but a play or modification. And thus spirit preserves [paradoxically] its radically immanent nature."[18]

Ken Wilber indicates that although this may seem to be an apparently trivial point, it is, in fact, vital to any discussion of how religion impacts science and vice versa. He points out that spirit is properly referred to not only in terms of it being "perfectly transcendent" but also as "perfectly immanent." If we fail to keep this fact in mind, it is easy to end up with conflicting statements regarding religion which too often result in such charges as "featureless pantheism," dogmatism or even "nonsensicality."

What I found fascinating was how he pointed out that there is a religious experience which can be evaluated scientifically just as there are psychological experiences that can be evaluated scientifically, and hence it is proper to speak of the science of religion just as we refer to the science of psychology. He claims that consciousness can be trained to apprehend the central features of religious experience; and he refers to this training as meditation or contemplation! He claims that religious experience is not "merely private knowledge." Rather, just as "Mathematical knowledge is public knowledge to all equally trained mathematicians; just so, contemplative knowledge is public knowledge to all equally trained contemplatives. The preposterous claim that all religious experience is private and noncommunicable is stopped dead by, to give only one example, the *transmission* of Buddha's enlightenment all the way down to the present-day Buddhist masters."[19]

Ken Wilber gives a bare bones definition of the scientific method, which he claims most general science texts agree with. He writes the "scientific method involves those knowledge-claims open to *experiential* validation or refutation."[20] This definition, however, does not refer either to the domain or the objects of the scientific method. Consequently, Ken Wilber says that with this definition, you can address not only the realms of biology and anthropology, but also such domains as psychology, history, sociology and even spirituality. For me, he clarifies this whole point when he writes: "If 'science' were restricted to 'physical-sensory' object-domains, then mathematics, logic, psychology, and sociology could not be called 'scientific,' in that the central aspects of those domains are non-sensory, non-empirical, non-physical, or meta-physical occasions."[21]

My understanding of the scientific method was based on the premise that the knowledge-claim being evaluated was to be tested using 'physical-sensory' evidence. My problem was with the definition I was using. I thought that 'experiential' evidence and 'physical-sensory' evidence meant the same thing. However, Ken Wilber makes it very clear that the use of the words 'experiential validation' in the generally accepted definition of the scientific method, does not restrict such validation to physical-sensory evidence! As an example, he points to the fact that testing the truth-value of a mathematical theorem is not based on sensory evidence, but rather on mental evidence. And he concludes that it is by using mental evidence, which can be checked by equally trained experts in their respective fields, that such subjects as mathematics, logic and psychology are correctly called sciences.

As I quoted earlier, in his book, *Mathematics and the Search for Knowledge,* Morris Kline makes a compelling statement regarding the essence of mathematics as compared to sense perceptions. He claims that mathematics "draws on the human mind and human reasoning to produce knowledge about our physical world that the average human being, even in Western culture, believes is acquired by the use of sense perceptions."[2] Until I read Kline's book I never appreciated the role mathematics played in the development of our scientific knowledge! After reading the book, I had a new respect for, almost a sense of awe towards mathematics. But I was still confused about the relationship between physics and mathematics.

As we have seen, Kline shows us that Newton's laws of motion were expressed mathematically and accepted by his colleagues, even though he could *not explain what matter or force meant!* Kline also points out that Maxwell's electromagnetic theory and the mathematical equations, which Maxwell posited, *had no relationship to physical reality.* And yet these mathematical equations have been the foundation, which has made possible the development of the many electrical and electronic wonders that we take for granted today, such as the TV, the cell phone and the iPOD. It is Kline's position that scientists have tried repeatedly, yet unsuccessfully, to explain electric and magnetic waves. No mechanical explanation has been found. He even says that 'fields' are simply a *crutch.* And that electrons *do not physically exist.* They are simply a variable in Maxwell's equations.

Kline asks what does it mean that we cannot reason in physical terms about such subjects as electromagnetic theory. Why are mathematical laws the only means that we have of mastering so much of the world we live in? He claims that this mystery, as to why mathematics is the foundation of our physical knowledge of the world, can be compared to "latter-day Delphic mysteries" to which the average person is uninitiated. He believes that because scientists are faced with so many natural mysteries that they are "only too glad to bury them under a weight of mathematical symbols, ***bury them so thoroughly that many generations of workers fail to notice the concealment.***"[22] (italics mine) When I reread this in connection with the new insights I had found in Ken Wilber's book, I began to understand why these aspects of physics do not seem to be taught to our students even today.

This role of mathematics in modern physics, extends to both Relativity and Quantum Mechanics; and has resulted in a major revision of classical mechanics. Relativity posits a four-dimensional, non-Euclidean universe. When I first read Einstein's book, *Relativity*, I had not a glimmer as to what he was saying, even though his book was listed as a 'Popular Exposition' on the title page. I simply did not understand relativity. And Einstein was attempting to make relativity understandable to the general public via this book! I asked my husband to explain to me what Einstein meant; and he did! But I still didn't understand, although my husband, the mathematician, understood what Einstein was trying to explain. Now as I reread Einstein's book I realize that I had a mental block.

I was trying to visualize the four-dimensional universe consisting of three space co-ordinates combined with a time co-ordinate. I was still in the dark ages as I tried to visualize this four-dimensional space-time continuum, and I didn't know it. Einstein points out that in his Special Theory of Relativity, the time co-ordinate "plays exactly the same role as the three space co-ordinates."[23] Of course, such a universe does not exist as a reality that we perceive. And one must simply look to the mathematics which express Einstein's theories and which are verified by our amazing accomplishments in outer space. A fact that I find particularly surprising is Einstein's words that "The special theory of relativity has crystalized from the Maxwell-Lorentz theory of electromagnetic phenomena."[24]

In quantum mechanics, the mathematics is rather advanced; and Morris Kline, who was a Professor Emeritus of Mathematics at New York University, indicates that it is not readily presentable. In his chapter: The Dissolution of Matter: Quantum Theory, of his book, *Mathematics and the Search for Knowledge*, he assures us that mathematics has played as important a role in quantum mechanics as it has in relativity and electromagnetic theory. Quantum theory is considered the most basic theory of matter that is available to us today. It deals with atomic and sub-atomic structures and has wide applicability in experimental physics.

Based on what I have learned from Morris Kline's book, I have tried to demonstrate that Newton's Law of Gravity, as well as the theories of Relativity and Quantum Mechanics, have as their foundation mathematical equations that may, in some cases, seem completely at variance with our sense perceptions of reality. Indeed, such *things* as electrons, quarks and a quanta of energy are only variables in the mathematical equations that apply to that area in physics in which they are used. Even electric and magnetic fields merely refer to the variables in the mathematical equations of their respective fields.

Space, time and matter are all distinct entities to me as I experience life each day. This, however, is not the case according to Einstein! His equations show that they form an organic whole, that space, time and matter are commingled! These are such astounding ideas that, the first time I ever came across them in Morris Kline's book, *Mathematics and the Search for Knowledge,* I was totally confounded and at a loss. However, when I ultimately read Ken Wilber's book, *Quantum Questions*, all of what I had previously read in Morris Kline's book came together. I finally understood that during those many years when I had difficulty in understanding physics, there was a good reason for it. *The reason was that many of the laws of physics were not based on reality.* But it was not until I read Ken Wilber's book that I finally appreciated what Morris Kline meant by those surprising statements about the lack of reality connected with the presentation of the laws of modern physics, that were sprinkled throughout his book.

In summation, Ken Wilber made, what was for me, at first reading, an absolutely astounding point that the physicist is not looking at *reality* itself. What he works with are the highly abstract mathematical equations in which *reality* is cloaked. In other words, they are looking at nothing but *shadows* of reality. This analogy is repeated throughout his compendium of the writings of the greatest physicists of modern times. For example, Sir James Jeans expresses it succinctly when he writes: "The essential fact is simply that *all* pictures which science now draws of nature, and which alone seem capable of according with observational fact, are *mathematical* pictures…They are nothing more than pictures – fictions if you like, if by fiction you mean that science is not yet in contact with ultimate reality."[25]

And Sir Arthur Eddington makes a similar statement: "Briefly the position is this. We have learnt that the exploration of the external world by the methods of physical science leads not to concrete reality but to a shadow world of symbols, beneath which those methods are unadapted for penetrating. Feeling that there must be more behind, we return to our starting point in *human consciousness* – the one centre where more might become known."[26]

Ken Wilber sums it up in a telling paragraph: "To put it in a nutshell: according to this view, physics deals with shadows, to go beyond shadows is to go beyond physics; to go beyond physics is to head toward the meta-physical or mystical – and *that* is why so many of our pioneering physicists were mystics. The new physics contributed nothing positive to this mystical venture, except a spectacular failure, **from whose smoking ruins the spirit of mysticism gently arose.**"[27] (bold emphasis mine)

TWELVE

THE INVISIBLE WALL

When I first heard of Centering Prayer, I wondered if it were one of those fads, like Transcendental Meditation (TM), which had become so popular in the States. Little did I suspect at that time how TM would grow! In an article in the Philadelphia Inquirer newspaper, dated Nov. 12, 2006, titled Philadelphia Region to Give Peace Palaces a Chance, writer Jeff Gammage says: "Yes, the Maharishi is *that* maharishi. The one-time guru to the Beatles now presides over the Global Country of World Peace, a Dutch village he converted into 'a country without borders for peace-loving people everywhere,' complete with its own currency." He goes on to point out that "While other '60's and '70's movements faded…TM prospered. Last year film director David Lynch announced creation of the Foundation for Consciousness-Based Education, through which he hopes to raise billions to train children in TM."

Jeff Gammage also points out that it is not a religion. He writes: "Despite its aura of Eastern mysticism, TM is not a religion. It's a practice – and a registered 501(c) (3) nonprofit organization. Thousands swear by it, meditating in twice-daily, 20-minute sessions. They say it enlivens the body and mind, producing a sense of bliss."

Back then it seemed likely to me that TM would last for a while and then ultimately fade away. I wondered if the same would also happen to Centering Prayer. However, since Centering Prayer sounded interesting and it occurred to me that it might provide some answers to my questions about my form of wordless, imageless prayer, I decided to learn more about it. I was interested to learn how it compared to what I had been hearing about TM. I took two different Centering Prayer, introductory workshops. The initial one was given by Gail Fitzpatrick-Hopler, a co-founder and the first full-time Executive Director of Contemplative Outreach. She gave a beautiful exposition, well presented in every aspect.

However, when the introductory workshop was over, I had one major concern. If I really understood Centering Prayer, and I wasn't sure if I did, it seemed to go in the face of the traditional Catholic teaching relative to where one begins the contemplative journey to union with God. The beginner in the spiritual journey normally starts with vocal and affective prayer. Their prayer life may, or may not, include discursive meditation on the life of Christ or on the many religious themes contained in various spiritual books, such as the *Imitation of Christ*, etc. When discursive meditation is not practiced, usually praying the rosary while meditating on each mystery is strongly recommended, rather than just concentrating on the words of the Our Father and Hail Marys themselves. In various religious orders certain prayers may be specified or the Divine Office may be said.

When the dark night of sense begins, however, the individual's prayer becomes dry and very difficult. If one has been practicing discursive meditation, this too becomes a problem. The person will be strongly tempted to give up prayer altogether. It is at this point on the spiritual journey that the individual needs a wise spiritual director to lead him/her onto the path of contemplation. It seemed to me that the starting point of Centering Prayer was that point in the spiritual journey at which the dark night of sense had already begun. To the best of my knowledge, this was not the traditional Catholic way of beginning the spiritual life!

Due to this concern of mine, I decided to take another Centering Prayer, introductory workshop with the hope that this issue would be resolved. This time it was given by Father Carl Arico, who was another co-founder, with Abbott Thomas Keating, of the Contemplative Outreach organization. I can still remember quite clearly how Fr. Carl taught us to employ our 'sacred word' in the softest way possible as if it were a feather gently alighting on some surface. The sacred word is similar to the mantra used in TM, but as Fr. Thomas explains in his book *Intimacy with God*: "The sacred word comes from the heart and reverberates in the imagination only momentarily, whereas a mantra or a concentrative process is designed to slow down the flow of thoughts."[1] The sacred word is employed by the person who is centering, whenever they find themselves attracted to any thought which is passing by on the stream of consciousness.

Fr. Carl did not address my concern during the general presentation, and there seemed to be little opportunity to express my question to him privately. On a table near where he was speaking, was Fr. Thomas Keating's classic book, *Open Mind, Open Heart, The Contemplative Dimension of the Gospel*. I glanced through it, but decided not to buy it because I had this thing about not buying a book unless I really felt that I was going to read it! And because I had difficulty in doing spiritual reading anyhow. Consequently, I was left with my concern and not certain what to think of Centering Prayer.

However, a short time later, as I was going to a nearby church to a funeral Mass for an AIDS victim, I suddenly decided, for some unknown reason, to see if I could buy the book, *Open Mind, Open Heart*, at a religious bookstore which was on my way to the church. When I got home I immediately started to read Fr. Thomas' book. I read it from cover to cover. I could barely put it down. When I finished reading it, I started to reread it, marking passages as I read it the second time.

As I read *Open Mind, Open Heart*, I started to feel as if a tremendous burden had been lifted from my shoulders. A burden that I had felt ever since I left Mt. St. Mary's Abbey in Wrentham, Massachusetts in 1952 because of health concerns. It was as if I had been wandering in the desert for 40 years, 1952 to 1992; and that reading Fr. Thomas' book had finally brought me into the Promised Land! His book was such a source of confirmation and encouragement to me. All my doubts about Centering Prayer and mystical contemplation were resolved!

What was this heavy burden that had been lifted from my shoulders? The only way I can describe it is to say that I felt as if I had been regularly bumping into an *invisible wall*. Each time it happened, I was taken aback. I felt like a bird who had just slammed into a glass patio door! I did not understand why I seemed to be coming from such a different place relative to the attitude of the people I met and the culture in which I lived. Contemplation seemed to me to be one of the most important things in this world, but no one I came in contact with seemed to be interested in it, or even to consider it of much value! I kept bumping into this attitude of indifference or, in some cases, of actual hostility against the idea of someone spending time in prayer.

And, if that wasn't bad enough, prayer was hard for me. When my wordless, imageless form of prayer became dry and God seemed to be absent, which was most of the time, I would question whether I was really praying or was I deluding myself into thinking that what I was doing had some value? I kept seeking for answers from different people and books. But I found no *guru* or book to help me. And each time I sought for help and answers I would bump again into that *invisible wall*.

In his third chapter of *Open Mind, Open Heart,* Fr. Thomas presents a history of contemplative prayer down through the centuries. As I read this chapter I came to understand what this *invisible wall* was and how it came about. He points out that *lectio divina* was the way both lay people as well as monastics prayed in the first centuries of the Christian Church. He describes *lectio* as follows: "The reflective part, pondering upon the words of the sacred text, was called *meditatio*, 'meditation.' The spontaneous movement of the will in response to these reflections was called *oratio*, 'affective prayer.' As these reflections and acts of will simplified, one moved on to a state of resting in the presence of God, and that is what is meant by *contemplatio*, 'contemplation.'....The term *mental prayer*, with its distinct categories, did not exist in Christian tradition prior to the sixteenth century."[2]

Around the twelfth century, the great schools of theology began and with it was the "birth of precise analysis in regards to concepts, division into genera and species, and definitions and classifications."[3] He points out that while this was an important development for humankind, it also had its unwanted side effects. Fr. Thomas goes on to say: "Unfortunately this passion for analysis in theology was later to be transferred to the practice of prayer and bring to an end the simple, spontaneous prayer of the Middle Ages based on *lectio divina* with its opening to contemplation."[4]

In discussing the spiritual marriage in Chapter Seven of this book, I mentioned that St. John of the Cross wrote of the three states that a person goes through to reach this transforming union with God. He refers to them as the purgative, illuminative and unitive stages. In the sixteenth century, this precise way of defining things resulted in mental prayer being divided into three distinct forms of prayer consisting of discursive meditation, affective prayer and contemplation. Nowadays, when we refer to the spiritual journey, this is what is usually meant.

Fr. Thomas indicates that these forms of prayer were no longer identified as part of a continuous sequence in one prayer setting. Instead, they were defined separately "each with its own proper aim, method and purpose. This division of the development of prayer into compartmentalized units entirely separate from one another **helped to further the incorrect notion** that contemplation was an extraordinary grace reserved for the few. The possibility of prayer opening out into contemplation tended to be regarded as very unlikely. The organic development of prayer toward contemplation **did not fit into the approved categories** and was therefore discouraged." (emphasis mine)[5]

Fr. Thomas writes that the attitude of Roman Catholic authorities regarding contemplation was also influenced by Quietism which was condemned in 1687 by Innocent XII as a type of false mysticism. At about the same time a less extreme form of Quietism, known as Semi-Quietism was condemned in France by Bishop Boussuet, who was the chaplain to the court of Louis XIV. As a result "reading about mysticism was frowned upon in seminaries and religious communities."[6] He states that even John of the Cross' writings became suspect and his editors modified or eliminated parts of his text. According to Fr. Thomas it was not until the twentieth century, 400 years after John of the Cross wrote his mystical treatise, that the unexpurgated text was published.

Jansenism was another heresy that flourished during the seventeenth century and was later condemned. Fr. Thomas writes that "it left behind a pervasive anti-human attitude that perdured throughout the nineteenth century and into our time…The pessimistic form of piety which it fostered spread with the emigres from the French Revolution to English-speaking regions including Ireland and the United States. Since it is largely from French and Irish stock that priests and religious in this country have come, Jansenistic narrowness, together with its distorted asceticism, has deeply affected the psychological climate of our seminaries and religious orders."[7] I have sometimes wondered what role the recognition and acknowledgment of this negative influence of Jansenism in the Catholic Church following the Second Vatican Council, played in the disillusionment and departure of so many devout individuals from the priesthood and religious life! And I wonder if this is not an example of how the 'sins of the fathers' are visited on their offspring; of how the beliefs of the early Jansenistic followers visited devastation down through the past few centuries on Christ's church!

In a later book, *Intimacy with God*, Fr. Thomas relates how, in talking to some of the guests who came to his monastery and who had been trying Eastern methods of meditation, he learned from many of them that they "had never heard that there was such a thing as Christian spirituality. They had not heard about it in their parishes or Catholic Schools if they attended one. Consequently, it did not occur to them to look for a Christian form of contemplative prayer or to visit Catholic monasteries."[8] I can relate to this because when I first entered the Trappists, I, too, knew nothing of Christian spirituality! It was only when I found that I could no longer pray as before, and after I found in the small library in the abbey, the book, *The Spiritual Life*, a treatise on Ascetical and Mystical Theology, by Adolphe Tanquerrey, S.S., D.D. that I first learned of Christian spirituality and mystical contemplation!

Relative to these visitors to the Monastery who were practicing Eastern methods of meditation, Fr. Thomas says of them "That many were having experiences very similar to what Christian tradition calls contemplation. Although I had studied Christian tradition deeply and had tried to practice it, I had found that when I talked about it in conferences to the monastic community, many of the monks were turned off. They didn't want to hear about contemplation. The priests who came to the guest house for retreats did not want to hear about it either. They had been trained in the seminary to think that contemplation belonged in cloisters and had no relation to what they were doing. If parish priests and professors in Catholic seminaries did not feel that contemplation was **suitable** for them or for their students, naturally lay folks did not either." (emphasis mine)[9] In his writings, Thomas Merton also mentioned more than once that the monks at Gethsemani did not share his enthusiasm for contemplation.

These attitudes in the seminaries, in the parishes and in the Catholic schools, including the universities, only served to exacerbate the effect on me of that *invisible wall* which I so frequently encountered. No one I knew, and none of the religious sisters and priests that I met seemed interested in the topic. Now that I was no longer in the Trappists there was no one to whom I could turn for encouragement and for spiritual guidance. And it was after I returned home from Mt. St. Mary's Abbey, that I really needed a *guru* to guide me. It now seems apparent to me that, while I was still in the Trappists, God had been preparing me for the future that lay ahead of me, and thus His spiritual consolations were almost continuous during those two years. It was only after I came home that the dark nights started in earnest. For 40 years I sought God and most of the time He was absent. I was in continuous doubt about the state of my soul.

In this same chapter on the history of contemplative prayer in *Open Mind, Open Heart*, Fr. Thomas speaks of the teachings of John of the Cross on the first stage of the contemplative journey, the night of sense. He emphasizes what happens when the night of sense begins and the importance of spiritual direction during this period. He likens the night of sense to a maturing process from childhood to adolescence in the spiritual life. His words were such a source of consolation to me as he discusses how the individual feels during this experience. Fr. Thomas paints a picture of what I felt, as he describes how a person feels when the senses and reason seem useless. He says that "One is more and more convinced that one can no longer pray at all."[10] And he also stresses that "People in this state have great anxiety about whether they are going backwards."[11]

When I finished reading this chapter, I began to realize how this *invisible wall* and heavy burden of which I speak, came about. I took the teachings of the Roman Catholic authorities seriously and what were they saying? As Fr. Thomas points out the post-Reformation teaching of the Church authorities was "**opposed to contemplation.**" (emphasis mine) [12] This was the dilemma with which I was faced. I felt a continuous call to contemplative prayer and yet the Church to which I belonged was *opposed to contemplation*.

Today, I look back and realize that this was one of the crosses that the Lord had chosen specifically for me. I was always uneasy about the idea of carrying my cross, and I often wondered if I could bear the crosses the Lord had planned for me. Now, in the last third of my life, as I look back on my spiritual journey, I realize that the Lord has never in that time given me a cross which was too heavy for me to bear. I sometimes wonder whether our heaviest crosses are not the fears that we experience relative to what life has in store for us. Today I see how these crosses have matured me in my faith, and brought me ever closer to my God and to union with the Godhead.

Reading the remainder of *Open Mind, Open Heart* impressed me greatly. There were so many words of wisdom, such insight into the contemplative journey and an obvious desire on the part of Fr. Thomas to bring as many people to contemplation as he could. He seemed to highlight all the key points that I had read so many times in the writings of John of the Cross, but could not seem to apply to myself. As a result of reading Fr. Thomas' book I found that

I was no longer concerned that Centering Prayer started the spiritual journey in a non-traditional place.

About a year or so later, I found that Fr. Thomas addressed this very question that I had been wondering about relative to Centering Prayer in his book, *Intimacy with God.* He writes: "Now the **delicate question** arises, 'Can we *begin* a life of prayer with Centering Prayer?' Tradition says that we should normally begin with discursive meditation and that we should not move beyond affective prayer unless we know God is calling us. The usual signs given by St. John of the Cross are not easy to verify in concrete cases." (first emphasis mine)[13] Father Thomas explains in his book. *Intimacy with God*, why he feels that, particularly in our age, starting the spiritual journey with Centering Prayer is a valid way to proceed. He points out that practicing *Lectio Divina*, which was the usual road for the monks to take in reaching contemplation, could be started at any one of the four stages. These four stages can be summed up as reading Sacred Scripture, reflecting, responding and resting in God. He maintains that those who start in the fourth stage of resting in God, normally, are subsequently attracted to the other three stages. In support of his position, he points to the many people who have, or are participating in the Contemplative Outreach programs. He writes: "The Contemplative Outreach network contains many witnesses to this statement's practical validity. From an initial access point in Centering Prayer, these people have been moved to fuller engagement with the whole Christian contemplative and scriptural tradition."[14]

He also indicates the advantages of starting Centering Prayer at any time during the spiritual journey. He mentions that one bishop told him how his practice of Centering Prayer had enhanced all his other spiritual devotions, giving the bishop new insight into the value and meaning of these other spiritual practices. Fr. Thomas goes on to make some very telling points. He writes: "If we could persuade people to start Centering Prayer, especially intellectuals who are not likely to experience contemplation without first disciplining their compulsion to reflect, all of the things they do would become better. Their daily prayer will be more interactive, their reflections will have the unction of the Holy Spirit, and their conversation will touch other people's hearts much more than before. We are talking here about love. This is also what distinguishes Centering Prayer from Eastern methods. Eastern methods are primarily concerned with awareness. Centering Prayer is concerned with divine love."[15]

Who is this Father Thomas Keating, OCSO? Why was he able to play such a dramatic role in my spiritual journey and in the lives of many others touched by his various ministries, including the founding of Contemplative Outreach and the many books he wrote? What is the background of this man who has become a key figure in renewing the Christian tradition of contemplative prayer?

Here and there among Fr. Thomas' books I found a number of references to his personal life. He was born about 1923 and when he was 21 he entered the Cistercian(Trappist) monastery in Valley Falls, Rhode Island. Both of his parents were opposed to his idea of becoming a monk. His father compared it to entering a tomb because of the way the Trappist monks were cut off from the world and from each other, and because the monks were allowed little contact with family and friends. His father believed that, if Fr. Thomas were to enter the monastery, that the money he had expended on Fr. Thomas's education at Yale and Fordham would be wasted. Because of this opposition by his parents and because the Trappists would not accept anyone under the age of 21 without written parental consent, Fr. Thomas had to postpone his plan to enter the Cistercian monastery until he reached the age of 21

Fr. Thomas explains why he selected the Trappists in his book, *Invitation to Love*. He writes: "In my understanding, contemplative prayer was the heart of the spiritual journey. At that time, an austere regime was considered the indispensable way to contemplation; hence I looked for the most difficult order I could find. I was willing to give up everything – family, friends, and comfort – in order to follow Christ into the desert."[16]

Why does Fr. Thomas refer to the Cistercians as the "most difficult order" that he could find? What were the beginnings of the Cistercian order and why are its members often referred to as Trappists? The Cistercian Order began in 1098 when the Monastery of Citeaux was founded by Abbot Robert of Mosleme for the purpose of restoring the original rule of St. Benedict. In 1112, St. Bernard of Clairvaux, who was about 22 years old, entered the Monastery of Citeaux, bringing with him 32 relatives, including five brothers. Three years later he was sent to found a new house which he called Clairvaux, the Valley of Light. During his 38 years as abbot, 300 monasteries were founded! St. Bernard is noted for his masterpiece, *Sermon on the Song of Songs,* which I mentioned in my chapter on Spiritual Marriage.

In the year 1119, Bernard was present at the first General Chapter of the order, convoked by the Abbot of Citeaux. As the result of Bernard's persuasive discourses concerning the revival of the primitive spirit, the General Chapter wrote the *charta caritatis* for the new Cistercian order, which Charter was subsequently approved by the then Pope. At its peak the Cistercian order had approximately 750 monasteries. However, the Cistercians went into decline, as both the ecclesiastical and secular powers began to appoint clerics of their own choice to the abbatical office, apparently influenced by the power and wealth which began to accumulate as the monasteries grew in size and importance,

It is fascinating to see how God turned evil into good. The Trappist order of monks arose from this corrupt policy! In the 17th century as part of this policy, Armand Jean de Rance was made a commendatory abbot as a mere child, for reasons which were apparently financial. He was not actually a member of the Abbey of Notre Dame de la Grande Trappe. However, as he grew up, he underwent a conversion which resulted in his working for a renewal of the original monastic practices of the Cistercians, such as monastic enclosure, silence, manual labor, abstinence from meat and a life devoted to prayer. These reform Cistercians came to be known as the Cistercian Order of the Strict Observance as distinct from the present day Cistercians of the Common Observance. As God would ordain, it was the monks of this Cistercian monastery of La Trappe, who would survive the destruction of many monasteries and the dispersal of the monks during the French Revolution. Ultimately, they regrouped and resumed their monastic life in common. These monks of the Cistercian Order of the Strict Observance and the foundations they started are commonly referred to as 'Trappists.'

It was in this order of Trappists, in St. Joseph's Abbey in Spencer, Massachusetts, that Fr. Thomas Keating had taken his vows. And in 1965, Fr. Thomas was elected abbot of Spencer Abbey, which is one of approximately 170 Trappist monasteries in existence today. Of these, 100 monasteries belong to the monks of the Cistercian Order of the Strict Observance and approximately 70 abbeys belong to the Trappistine nuns. It is my understanding that these 70 monasteries of nuns have a unique position in the Church in that they serve with the monks on the Cistercian staff of the order in Rome and they are equally part of the order.

At that time, when Fr. Thomas became abbot, the Second Vatican Council was ending and religious were directed to reevaluate their lifestyle. He points out that it was the first time in 900 years that the Cistercian observances were being questioned and, for many monks, it was a time of crises. It seemed to me, reading between the lines of what Fr. Thomas has written, that it was also a time of severe trials for him and that these trials lasted many years. He indicates that the abbot was the final arbitrator in all discussions. Was this responsibility a heavy burden for him? I think so. He gives an insight into his feelings when he refers to the stress that major superiors were experiencing due to the "profound upheavals in the religious life following the Second Vatican Council."[17]

In the middle of the 1970's, Fr. Thomas noticed that many young people were turning east to seek something that seemed to be missing in their lives. He asked himself: "Why were the young disciples of Eastern gurus, Zen roshis, and teachers of TM, who were coming to the abbey in the 1970's for dialogue, experiencing significant spiritual experiences without having gone through the penitential exercises that the Trappist order required?"[18] In addition he was concerned that many Catholic young people had turned to the east for spiritual direction. Thinking on this problem, Fr. Thomas decided to put this question before the community of monks at Spencer Abbey: "Could we put the Christian tradition into a form that would be accessible to people in the active ministry today and to young people who have been instructed in an Eastern technique and might be inspired to return to their Christian roots if they knew there was something similar in the Christian Tradition?"[19] In response to this challenge, Fr. William Meninger wrote up a method that he called the 'Prayer of the Cloud' based primarily on the contents of the book, the *Cloud of Unknowing*. He proceeded to teach this method to priests on retreat at the Monastery and it was well received.

Subsequently, Fr. Basil Pennington, another monk at Spencer Abbey, put together an Introductory Workshop based on Father Meninger's work. He presented this workshop for the first time at a large Retreat House in

Connecticut for a group of provincials of various religious congregations, both men and women. Fr. Thomas points out that Fr. Meninger's method, which he had called 'Prayer of the Cloud', was rechristened Centering Prayer by these retreat participants. Fr. Thomas felt that they were probably influenced in this choice by the writings of the late Fr. Thomas Merton.

In the fall of 1981, Fr. Thomas resigned as abbot of Spencer Abbey and retired to their foundation in Snowmass, Colorado. At that time he had no plans to teach Centering Prayer. In the summer of 1982 he went to the Lama Foundation in New Mexico. A workshop was being given by Ram Dass who immediately invited Fr. Thomas to speak to the group. During his dialogue with the workshop participants, Fr. Thomas was impressed by the fact that a large number of the participants were Catholics. Talking to them he discovered that "Many of them were disaffected from the religion of their youth because of the legalistic and overmoralistic teaching that many had received in their local parishes and Catholic schools; they now felt spiritually enriched by their experiences in Buddhism and Hinduism."[20]

In August 1983, Lama invited Fr. Thomas to offer a program at its Intensive Studies Center. For some time Fr. Thomas had been interested in offering a "Christian contemplative retreat that would be comparable to a Zen sesshin, with a significant amount of time spent in silent meditation…"[21] He states that it turned out to be a "watershed" experience and that half of the original Lama retreatants became pillars of the Contemplative Outreach network. Subsequently, with the assistance of New York's Cardinal John O'Connor and Bishop Joseph O'Keefe, they were able to fund a pilot program for the archdiocese of New York. Their first Centering Prayer event was a workshop at Holy Trinity Church in New York, which was attended by over 350 people. After the first workshop, additional workshops and support groups started to form and flourish.

Since that time, Contemplative Outreach has grown throughout the United States. As a result of this growth it became necessary to divide the United States into 13 outreach regions, including Alaska and Hawaii. The international outreach includes Australia, Israel, two countries in Africa, five countries in Asia, four countries in Central and South America, five countries in Europe and eight countries in North America and the Caribbean. Fr. Thomas has written approximately 12 books, most of which were completed after he "retired" to Snowmass, CO. in 1981. The majority of his books address the spiritual life, the contemplative journey, and the role of Centering Prayer and *Lectio Divina* in renewing the contemplative dimension of the Gospel. Some of his books were developed subsequent to his giving a number of seminars on the practice of Centering Prayer to participants with different levels of experience in contemplation.

In the spring of 1992, after my initial readings of Fr. Thomas' book, *Open Mind, Open Heart*, I wrote to him to thank him and to let him know what a tremendous source of consolation and encouragement his book was to me. Then, in the spring of 1993, a newcomer to our parish joined our Little Rock Bible Study group. She had approached one of our parish priests, asking him various questions. In response, he suggested that she join one of our Bible Study groups. After the meetings she started talking to me. I soon learned that she was well versed in Scripture. She later told me that she assumed that, since I was the facilitator and since the parish priest had suggested that she join the Bible Study, that I would have all the answers she was seeking.

However, the answers she was seeking were not about the Scripture that we were studying, but rather about mystical phenomena. She told me that she was having visions of Our Lord and other figural images. After talking to her many times without seeming to help her, I thought to myself that it might be a good idea to seek some help from

Fr. Thomas Keating. I first thought that she and I could go together to Snowmass, CO. to see Fr. Thomas, but that didn't seem too likely. I was anxious to help her and I didn't want to give up on the idea of talking to Fr. Thomas about her. So I asked her permission to talk to Fr. Thomas without her being present. She acquiesced. Tending toward synergism wherever possible, I thought to myself that if I were to go to Snowmass, CO., Fr. Thomas could give me guidance not only for this woman in my Bible Study group, but also, that I could seek Fr. Thomas' direction in my own contemplative journey.

When I contacted Fr. Thomas, he was most cordial about a visit. However, the Monastery was crowded at this time with visitors and Fr. Thomas suggested that I might be able to get accommodations at a family nearby who sometimes hosted overflow guests from the Monastery. I decided to stay a few days and incorporate my visit with Fr.Thomas as part of a private retreat. I would never have gone to see him just for myself. It was only because I wanted help and advice about this woman in my Little Rock Bible Study group that I was willing to travel such a long distance. However, when I visited with Fr. Thomas I realized how important it was for me to talk to him. Relying solely on books is not enough. There are times in the spiritual journey when advice from an experienced and knowledgeable person can make all the difference in the world!

After my meeting with Fr. Thomas at the Monastery was ended, he suggested that I might want to attend a week long seminar in Chrysalis House in Warwick, New York which was coming up in the near future. I did attend. Fr. Thomas was there the whole week. David Frennete and Mary McCarthy, who were members at that time of the contemplative live-in lay community at Chrysalis House, were also there. It was wonderful to get such an opportunity to see Fr. Thomas saying Mass, giving conferences, and eating with us the vegetarian meals which they served.

Everyone also had an opportunity for a private meeting with Fr. Thomas.

Sometime later, as I was watching golf on the TV with my husband, it suddenly came to me that I should start a Centering Prayer group in Notre Dame parish on Long Island, where I lived at the time. It was the last thing I wanted to do! I am basically a very quiet and shy person and the thought of leading a prayer group left me cold. It was easier with the Bible Study because I had, as it were, an outline to follow and questions to be discussed as well as a taped lecture we could all listen to. Despite my aversion to starting a prayer group, I finally decided to go ahead with the project. I approached the pastor about it and about needing space somewhere in the Church facilities to hold the meetings. I thought that the Centering Prayer meetings should be held every week. However, because of space constraints we ended up having the meetings twice a month.

For the first meeting we had over 25 people, which was a large number for a Centering Prayer group. When I wrote to Fr. Thomas telling him about it, he suggested that we consider breaking the group up into three distinct sections, which we then did during the discussion part of the prayer meeting. I had told Fr. Thomas that I planned to use the "Lessons from Our Lord" contained in the book, *I am your JESUS of MERCY*, which Dr. Gianna Sullivan had received from Jesus while she was still living in Scottsdale, AZ. Fr. Thomas made no objection to my selection of reading material.

However, a few months after we had started the Centering Prayer group, one of the members of the group phoned me and told me that some of them were having difficulty with the book I had selected. They found it hard to believe that the *Lessons* were the words of Jesus. This upset me, for I loved the *Lessons* dearly, and I felt strongly that they formed a complete treatise on the spiritual life leading to the Transforming Union. However, after prayer and discernment, I decided to stop using the *Lessons*. This decision was very difficult for me, but I think it was the Lord's will at the time, as evidenced by the fact that this Centering Prayer group continues twice a month in Notre Dame parish to this day.

Then, in the fall of the year 2000, I started to feel that the Lord wanted me to do something for Him on the World Wide Web. I had absolutely no idea what I might do, or even if this inclination really was coming from the Lord. While I had had a desktop computer since I retired in 1988, I had only been on the internet once and that was early on. I did not have internet access in the year 2000 and I had not learned to work with Windows. I was still using the older DOS operating system. I decided that the first thing I should do was to learn more about the internet, about Windows and possibly replace my working computer with a new one. After thinking more on this subject, and investigating the various desktop computers on the market, I finally bought a new one in June of 2001 and started to subscribe to an Internet Service Provider.

The first month I used the computer I had no end of problems. I kept calling the service technician. Each time, after the technician and I worked for an extended period of time during a phone consultation, the computer would start to work again. Finally, it dawned on me that I must have an intermittent hardware problem. When I finally convinced Compaq of this fact, they agreed to arrange to have me ship the computer back to them. It was, indeed, the computer and after they replaced a chip, I had no more problems for the first two years. While I already was conversant with computers, I still found that I had a lot of catching up to do with the latest Windows operating system and all the new software that came with it.

At about the same time, I started thinking about learning how to design a web site and how to upload it to the internet. However, I still didn't know what I would put on it! Then I started thinking about the *Lessons* that I had attempted to use in the early '90's with my Centering Prayer group. I realized that they were not available on the internet, as Dr. Gianna Sullivan did not have a web site. After getting her permission to publish these *Lessons* on the internet; and after seeking Fr. Thomas' advice, I decided to create my own web site. Upon further thought, I decided that not only would I publish these *Lessons* on the internet, but I would also try to establish a contemplative prayer group on the internet and use the *Lessons* for discussion at each meeting. I am now calling it the *JESUS of MERCY Contemplative Prayer Group.*

During the prayer meeting participants are urged to pray for 20 minutes using one of three forms of prayer: 1. Praying the rosary slowly, 2. Centering, or 3. Using the meditation method of John Main. The meeting includes a discussion of the selected *Lesson* as well as any questions about contemplative prayer, Centering Prayer, etc. that the participants may ask. I feel that the many difficulties that the *invisible wall* created for me, and the fact that there is still a large anti-contemplative residue in our culture, together with all of the reading I have done on mystical contemplation, will help me as a prayer group facilitator. A period of socializing is also included. The real-time contemplative prayer group communicates using Yahoo's Messenger, which is free, together with Yahoo's instant messaging or voice feature. So far I have tried having a prayer group a couple of times using instant messaging. It seems a very promising use for the World Wide Web.

THIRTEEN

MYSTICAL CONTEMPLATION

When I think of mystical contemplation, there are two scriptural passages that come most often to my mind. The text of the first one is to "pray without ceasing." (1 *Th.* 5:17) I often puzzled about these words. How is it possible to do such a thing? One answer I was told was that, if one made a morning offering of one's whole day, then everything one did that day would be a prayer. While I think the Morning Offering is an excellent prayer and, assuming we mean what we say, I believe that it signals our good intentions to God. But does that, of itself, make our day into a prayer? What if we were to commit a grievous sin? That certainly cannot be classified as a prayer. I felt that there must be a more profound meaning in this passage which urges us to pray without ceasing. But I couldn't imagine saying vocal prayers all day long, either!

The other scriptural passage consists of the words of St. Paul: "I am crucified with Christ: nevertheless I live, yet not I, but Christ liveth in me." (Gal. 2:20) The Divine Indwelling of the Holy Trinity is a truth of the Christian faith. Some have suggested that St. Paul's words refer to this Divine Indwelling. However, the fact that God dwells within us did not seem to me to fully explain the words of St. Paul.

As I pondered on these two passages from Scripture and read numerous books on contemplation, I finally came to the conclusion that only when contemplation becomes our normal state, that is, the mystical marriage has taken place, that these passages become fully operative in our every day life. To me, to fulfill these Scriptural ideals is only possible if we enter upon and persevere in the contemplative journey.

Contemplation can be defined in many ways. In Chapter Two of *Open Mind, Open Heart*, in which Fr. Thomas Keating addresses the dimensions of contemplative prayer, he gives a marvelous definition. He writes: "Contemplative prayer is the world in which God can do anything. To move into that realm is the **greatest adventure**. It is to be open to the Infinite and hence to infinite possibilities. Our private, self-made worlds come to an end; a new world appears within and around us and the impossible becomes an everyday experience. Yet the world that prayer reveals is barely noticeable in the ordinary course of events." (emphasis mine)[1] He goes on to give another definition of contemplation, saying that, while all prayer is inspired by the Spirit within us, he feels that it is: "more accurate to reserve the term *prayer in the Spirit*, for that prayer in which the inspiration of the Spirit is given directly to our spirit without the intermediary of our own reflections or acts of will. In other words, the Spirit prays in us and we consent. The traditional term for this kind of prayer is contemplation." [2]

Self-denial is never a pleasant thought, but it is required of the Christian who wishes to follow Christ. But what sort of self-denial are we talking about? Fr. Thomas tells us what form of self-denial is required in contemplative prayer when he writes the following: "Jesus said, 'Unless you deny your inmost self and take up the cross, you cannot be my disciple.'(Mark 8:34) Denial of our *inmost* self includes detachment from the habitual functioning of our intellect and will, which are our inmost faculties. This may require letting go not only of ordinary thoughts during prayer, but also of our most devout reflections and aspirations insofar as we treat them as indispensable means of going to God."[3]

However, Christ also says that not only must you deny yourself, but you must also take up your cross. St. Paul speaks of the cross when he says "I am crucified with Christ." But then he follows that with "Christ liveth in me." (Gal. 2:20) It would seem that the contemplative's cross involves both the *night of sense* and the *night of spirit*, which the contemplative normally experiences prior to the transforming union. Is there another night after the *night of the spirit*? Fr. Thomas indicates that the contemplative can go through multiple nights of sense and spirit. However, in his gem of a book, *Fruits and Gifts of the Spirit*, he speaks of a further night, the *night of self.*

In the past I tended to think that the transforming union was the ultimate goal in this life. Now I realize that it is just the beginning of a further stage in the contemplative's journey. In a chapter on transforming union in his book, *Invitation to Love*, Fr. Thomas concludes with the following words: "Transforming union is the goal of the **first part** of the Christian spiritual journey…The principle means of reaching the transforming union is the personal love of Christ. The next part of the journey is to learn the meaning of Jesus' words, 'The Father and I are one'(John 10:30), and the consequences of his prayer, "That they may be one in us.'" (John 17:21) (emphasis mine)[4]

In his book, *Fruits and Gifts of the Spirit*, Fr. Thomas again mentions that, after the transforming union occurs, the contemplative has a further distance to go on the spiritual journey. He concludes his book with a beautiful poem titled 'The Night of Self.' He writes: "There remains the movement from divine union to unity, the letting go of one's self-identity as a fixed point of reference, a passage that might be called the Night of Self."[5] I found the last two verses of his poem particularly significant. Fr. Thomas writes:

"When all anxious seeking stops
Unity begins.
But every time I act

even if to pray
Unity dissolves.

"When all striving ceases
I awaken to behold
Ever-present Awareness
Keeping silent watch."[6]

In his book, *Open Mind, Open Heart*, Fr. Thomas not only tells us what contemplation and Centering Prayer are, but he also tells us what *contemplation and Centering Prayer are not.* Surprisingly enough, the things he identifies as not belonging to mystical contemplation are precisely the very things that the popular mind associates with contemplation! The first thing he points out is that it is not an exercise or method intended to relax you. In the previous chapter we talked about Transcendental Meditation (TM) and quoted the Philadelphia Inquirer journalist, Jeff Gammage, who wrote that TM produces a sense of *bliss*. In his book, *Intimacy with God*, Fr. Thomas points out that "Centering Prayer is not a shortcut to bliss."[7] He writes about how he read a thesis by a young man who advised people to use Centering Prayer and other forms of Eastern meditation to reduce their anxiety. Fr. Thomas relates how he wrote to this man that "Centering Prayer will reduce anxiety perhaps for the first three months. But once the unconscious starts to unload, it will give you more anxiety than you ever had in your life."[8]

In Fr. Thomas' list of what contemplation is not, the second point he makes is that the charismatic gifts should not be confused with contemplation. Charismatic gifts are given for the good of others, except for the gift of tongues which is for the benefit of the individual. Fr. Thomas says that these gifts "include the interpretations of tongues, prophecy, healing, administration, the word of wisdom, and inspired teaching. Prophecy can exist in people who are not holy at all.…According to Catholic tradition, the straight and narrow path of contemplative prayer is the surest path to holiness.

The charismatic gifts are accidental or secondary to that path."[9] Another interesting statement that he makes is: "All prophecy is conditional. God does not commit himself to follow through on His threats. He reserves the right to change His mind if people respond by amending their lives. The prophet often gets left holding the bag; it's one of his occupational hazards."[10] As I read what the modern day prophets had to say about the coming chastisements related to the Second Coming and the Book of Revelations, I had to make a strong effort to keep this point of Fr. Thomas' in mind.

The third thing that Fr. Thomas says is not part of contemplative prayer, is parapsychological *phenomena.* Some of the examples he cites of psychic *phenomena* include precognition, out-of-body experiences and levitation. He also includes in this list, locutions and visions. Fr. Thomas mentions that the Church teaches that these types of gifts should be avoided, if at all possible, because of the danger of pride.

The fourth thing he says is not part of contemplative prayer is mystical *phenomena.* Fr. Thomas lists visions and locutions in this category also. However, in this case they are graces given by God. In the previous paragraph he does not go into the causes of psychic *phenomena*, but they can be caused by Satan according to John of the Cross. Fr. Thomas writes: "By mystical phenomena, I mean bodily ecstasy, external and internal visions, external words, words spoken in the imagination and words impressed upon one's spirit when any of these are the work of God's special grace in the soul."[11] To the average lay person these special graces would all be considered part of mystical contemplation! Yet, Fr. Thomas says they are not!

Fr. Thomas indicates that John of the Cross in his book, *Ascent of Mt. Carmel*, made an exhaustive list of spiritual *phenomena* and that John of the Cross "commands his disciples to reject them all."[12] John of the Cross' teachings are often considered very strict and demanding. But it is very important that his words be read in the context of all of his writings on contemplation. For example, in the *Ascent of Mt. Carmel*, John of the Cross explains how the contemplative soul must ever be guided by faith and he stresses how the soul must be void and in a state of detachment from all created things "so that, however many supernatural experiences it may have, it will ever remain as it were detached from them and in darkness."[13] In a later chapter, John of the Cross goes on to use very tough language. He writes: "And when at last he is reduced to nothing, which will be the greatest extreme of humility, spiritual union will be wrought between the soul and God, which in this life is the greatest and highest attainable. This consists not, then, in refreshment and in consolations and spiritual feelings, but in a living death of the Cross, both as to sense and as to spirit – that is, both inwardly and outwardly."[14] Based on my experience, it is my opinion that Centering Prayer is one of the best, if not the best way, of learning and practicing this detachment and nothingness which John of the Cross emphasizes so strongly!

However, in sharp contrast to this very strong language quoted in the previous paragraph, John of the Cross describes the fruits of detachment from all these spiritual experiences. He says: "Not only is it (the soul) not deprived of these communications (such as imaginary visions) and blessings which they cause within it, but it is much better prepared to receive them with greater abundance, clearness, liberty of spirit and simplicity."[15] Moreover, John of the Cross speaks in elegant language of an experience which a contemplative may have relative to a spiritual understanding of God. He writes of this knowledge that "the delight caused in it (the soul) by the kind that relates to God is comparable to nothing whatsoever, and there are no words or terms wherein it can be described…when the soul, after a most lofty manner, has a perception of some attribute of God – of His omnipotence, of His might, of His goodness and sweetness, etc.;…Inasmuch as this is **pure contemplation**, the soul clearly sees that there is no way wherein it can say aught concerning it, save to speak in general terms, of the abundance of delight and blessing which it has felt." (emphasis mine)[16]

Another important point that Fr. Thomas makes in his book, *Open Mind, Open Heart*, about mystical *phenomena* relates to the problems associated with understanding them. He writes: "External visions and voices can be misunderstood. Even saints have misunderstood what God has said to them. Divine communications of an intelligible kind have to be filtered through the human psyche and one's cultural conditioning."[17] He further states that "God does not bind Himself to the literal interpretations of His messages."[18] This is one of my problems. Sometimes, when I read what these visionaries have identified as being words from God or Our Lady, and particularly when something bothers me about the message, I have to remind myself to discern carefully, making sure that I am reading within the context of the whole set of messages and that I am not taking the more symbolic elements too literally. This continues to be a slow learning process for me!

John of the Cross makes similar statements. He writes: "And herein lies a great delusion, for revelations or locutions which are of God do not always turn out as men expect or as they imagine inwardly. And thus they must never be believed or trusted blindly, even though they are known to be revelations or answers or sayings of God."[19] Later he writes specifically of "formal words." These are interior words that the soul experiences without the senses being involved. They are spoken to the individual's spirit formally by a third person. An example would probably be an apparition in which Mary, the mother of God, gives messages to a visionary. John of the Cross writes: "The soul, then, must take no account of what these words may express, nor attach any importance to them, whether the spirit from which they come be good or evil. But the words **must be repeated to an experienced confessor, or to a discreet and learned person**, that he may give instruction and see what it is well to do, and impart advice; and the soul must behave, with regard to them, in a resigned and negative way. And if such an expert person cannot be found, it is better to attach no importance to these words and to repeat them to nobody." (emphasis mine)[20]

Elmer O'Brien, S.J. wrote the book, the *Varieties of Mystic Experience*, which is both an anthology as well as an interpretation of the experiences of mystics from the third to the seventeenth centuries. In his introduction he discusses the different literary forms which were used by the mystics to record their experiences. Fr. O'Brien indicates that the historian's task is complicated by the many different literary variations employed, such as general exhortations, pastoral homilies, theological treatises, poems, confessions, etc. He makes a provocative point regarding one particular literary form, personal advice.

Fr. O'Brien states that the *Cloud of Unknowing*, as well as the works of John of the Cross and Teresa of Avila, are all written in the form of personal advice. He notes that they have one particular similarity in common. That is, they were all written for the benefit of one or a small number of mystics. He points out that the advice is personal and thereby limited in two ways. Fr. O'Brien writes: "only the amount of experience – limited – of the author which is relevant to the need – limited – of the one advised is described. It is one of the less pleasant curiosities of religious history that the writings of such authors should have come to be esteemed as complete Baedekers of the mystical life."[21]

In his book, *Intimacy with God*, Fr. Thomas describes how he studied the Christian contemplative tradition and how this affected the development and the teaching of Centering Prayer. He points out that "Centering Prayer is a re-expression, in a form adapted to our time, of the apophatic tradition that was initially developed by the Desert Fathers and reported to Cassian, but has its roots much earlier. It is already adumbrated in St. Paul."[22] He goes on to analyze and explain the role played by the teachings of Cassian, Abba Isaac, Pseudo-Dionysius, the author of the *Cloud of Unknowing*, St Francis DeSales, St. Jane de Chantal and John of the Cross' book, the *Living Flame of Love*, in the development and teaching of Centering Prayer.

Fr. Thomas makes a very important statement, although a less critical observation than the words of Fr. O'Brien, relative to how the authorities on mystical contemplation should be evaluated. Fr. Thomas writes: "We cannot undiscriminatingly trust any of the spiritual masters. Each is conditioned by his or her time and culture, at least in some degree. Looking at the tradition, we have to know how to read the Fathers and to bring them into critical relationship with later writers and with modern psychology, exercising caution regarding exhortations of writers who did not have that knowledge."[23]

In the very next chapter of *Intimacy with God*, Fr. Thomas discusses the role of the rosary in contemplative prayer. He points out that it originated in the early Middle Ages and that, in a way, the "rosary became the office of lay persons. It also gradually became for some a method leading to contemplative prayer."[24] He points out how in the various apparitions of Our Lady in the last two centuries, Mary keeps asking us to say the rosary. He makes a most interesting comment regarding Our Lady's request. Fr. Thomas writes: "maybe this is just my prejudice as a contemplative, but in my view what she means is not only to pray, but to pray in such a way as to become a contemplative. In other words, 'Say the rosary in a contemplative way.' **Thus it is**

contemplative prayer that she is primarily requesting." (emphasis mine)[25]

As I mentioned earlier in this book, as an adult I was turned off by various apparitions and alleged supernatural happenings. In particular, I didn't understand what their purpose was. I started to believe that there was too much gimmickery involved in some of the apparitions. For example, I mistakenly thought that it was part of the message of Fatima that if we went to Mass and received Holy Communion for five consecutive Saturdays the result would be that we would be saved! It seemed to me that such an alleged promise, which did not seem to require a change of heart, lacked real substance. Then when the year 1960 came and went with no mention of the third secret of Fatima, I was further disillusioned even though I knew that the Bishop of Fatima, after seven years of investigation into the events of Fatima had been conducted, declared that they were worthy of credence. Thereafter, numerous Popes also indicated their personal belief in the validity of these apparitions at Fatima.

Now, having read a number of books on Fatima, notably John M. Haffert's book, *Deadline, The Third Secret of Fatima*, and Francis Johnston's book, *Fatima, The Great Sign*, I have made a complete about face. For one thing, I never understood that when Our Lady asked us to attend Mass and receive the Eucharist on the first Saturday of the month for five consecutive months, she also asked that we go to confession, that we recite five decades of the rosary, and that we keep Mary company while we spend fifteen minutes meditating on the mysteries of the rosary on each of those five Saturdays. This was to be done as an act of reparation to Our Lady. If we did this, she promised that she would assist us at the hour of our death with all the graces necessary to salvation. This does not necessarily mean that we will be saved, for in the end it is always up to us. In other words, it was not a 'gimmickery' kind of thing. Further, Mary was asking us, as well as the three young visionaries, for daily recitation of the rosary. As I read the two books on Fatima, the one by John Haffert and the other by Francis Johnston, I came to understand that Mary was calling each of us to a true metanoia. Moreover, I now strongly believe, as Fr. Thomas suggests, that Mary, as she repeatedly asks us to pray the rosary, is in essence, calling us all to pursue the path of contemplation

As I indicated, I read the complete set of the *I am your JESUS of MERCY* books and was very strongly affected by them. The thing that impressed me most was the emphasis on contemplative prayer and the role of repentance on the contemplative journey. This Divine call to contemplation is also stressed in the Vassula Ryden messages, and she herself has been placing emphasis on it these later years. That is why I feel so strongly about the inspired messages and teachings of both Dr. Gianna Sullivan and the Greek Orthodox mystic, Mrs. Vassula Ryden. In the following chapters I will be addressing both of these visionaries with a particular emphasis on the messages that seem to me to relate to the call to the contemplative journey and to the Second Coming.

FOURTEEN

"RECOGNIZABLY JEWISH"

Once again I went to visit my charismatic friend, Sister Nancy Mullen. I don't remember much about our conversation. However, I do remember Sister Nancy mentioning the *True Life in God* (TLIG) messages received by Vassula Ryden from the Holy Trinity. She showed me a copy of one of Vassula's messages in the handwriting Vassula uses when under dictation from one of the three Divine Persons or from St. Mary, as the Orthodox refer to Our Lady. As usual, I had a similar reaction to the ones I had when I first heard from Sister Nancy about the Medjugorje apparitions and later about the Scottsdale apparitions. I was skeptical! Also, I was bothered by the similarity with what seemed like automatic handwriting, although I did not know it by that name then. Again, I thought to myself, if this is from God, I will surely hear more about it.

Although, I don't remember the details of how I next heard of Vassula, I do remember going to hear her speak in Hempstead, Long Island, N.Y. It was a delightful experience. She spoke of her angel, Daniel; of how she came to know him as a friend and protector; and of how he prepared her to meet her God. The following year Vassula was again invited to speak in Hempstead. I had been so impressed by Vassula's presentation the previous year, that for the second meeting, I invited some women from our bible study group to come with me to hear her. However, I didn't feel inclined to buy any of Vassula's books which were for sale, at cost, at the entrance to the meeting room. I still had not come to terms with the strong scepticism and wariness which I feel whenever I hear of such alleged supernatural events. This despite the fact that I was very impressed with Vassula, the person. However, one of my companions did buy a Vassula book. When we left for home, the woman turned to me and said that she would not be able to read the book, and she insisted that I take it!

When I got home I started to read Vassula's messages, titled *True Life in God* (TLIG). They captivated me! I had never in my life read anything quite like it before. Again, as with Gianna Sullivan's *Lessons from Our Lord*, I found myself filled with awe and wonder as I read the messages over and over again. I ultimately read all of the messages from Notebook 1 to Notebook 108. The True Life in God messages have been published in over 40 languages. These messages have just been republished in a leather bound volume of more than eleven hundred pages. As I write this I wonder if there is any way I can possibly describe the magnificence that I found contained in these messages. The answer is that I can't even begin to try to come near expressing what I feel in my own words! But I can present the words which many others have used.

First and foremost let me cite some of the expressions that God, himself, as well as Our Lady, use to describe these messages. In a book titled *The Two Witnesses* by Father Michael O'Carroll, C.S.Sp. he quotes Our Lady as follows: "My Vassula, listen to Me very carefully now. The Lord, in His Mercy, has given you this Treasure *(The Message: True Life in God)* directly from His Sacred Heart."[1] In the Messages God, the Father, makes an unusually beautiful statement: "in these times of Grace, I come with Mercy, and *I address you with poetry;"*[2] (italics mine). Yahweh makes another very profound statement in explaining why He is not recognized as the author of these messages. He says: "without the Holy Spirit who transcends thought, and who is beyond all the constellations of light put together, the utterances and the expressions of Wisdom in My Word will remain hidden from you; the Holy Spirit alone gives the necessary light in your mind to understand the heavenly utterances, otherwise My Words will remain sealed and closed; this is the reason *why so many of you do not recognize Me in this Ode of Love;"*[3](italics mine)

What does Vassula herself say of these Messages? In the front of Vassula's book, *My Angel Daniel*, in a Presentation by Robert J. Carroll, US Foreign Service Officer, Retired, he says that Vassula "was given to understand that this body of messages constitute a 'love letter' to each of us. Thus the personal touch of giving them in handwritten form is fitting."[4] I have often meditated on the thought that God must love us. Why else would He have allowed His Son to die for us? However, for some reason, the idea that God could love us so much that He would write Hymns of Love to us, is beyond my comprehension! It simply boggles my mind!

Why is God giving us these messages? God the Father tells us that He wants us to come back to Him. He bemoans our apostasy and He predicts that His: "Love Hymn will grow into a river and this river will grow into a sea of Love." (TLIG 5-15-92) We can see how this is starting to happen. For example, in the December 2006 TLIG Magazine, a 23-year old Polish youth named Aleksander, who was enrolled in a joint computer science and law degree program at a nearby university, writes: "Everything I earned I spent on having a good time; partying, music, alcohol, drugs, sex. Getting 'wasted' at parties was not unusual." However, this lifestyle took a toll on his health and he ultimately reached a point where he felt that he couldn't even study for his exams. In desperation, he prayed to God for help. He writes: "The next day, looking through some web sites on the internet I chanced upon a web page with the TLIG Messages. I started to read and began to be totally immersed in them. Something amazing began to happen. I felt that what I was reading was written just for me. I didn't even have to replace Vassula's name with my own. I just knew God was talking to me, showing me the kind of life I was leading. It was the day when God started my conversion."

A little further on, he writes that "Soon I was able to take a decision to abandon my style of living and connected with it worldly ambitions…From then on God has been strengthening my faith and my love for Him and for fellow men by giving me Himself daily in the Eucharist." Aleksander has now changed his course of study at the University to theology.

There is an interesting testimony on the TLIG web site page, which lists Testimonies from Clergy and Religious. Fr. Robert Hughes, SM, San Jose, CA, USA, Jan. 1996, expresses exactly what I feel about these TLIG Messages, but I didn't feel qualified to make such a strong statement. He says: "The messages contained in TLIG are unique, extraordinary and very special. They reveal to us the most exalted treasures in the Sacred Heart of Jesus hidden in the past and reserved in a special way for our time. **They are the most important private revelations ever made."** (emphasis mine)

In the beginning of the handwritten version of Vol. 12, there is a statement by Fr. Dimitri Mottier, who is responsible for a small parish and for the Swiss eparchy of the Celetic Orthodox Church. He is also a practicing chemistry teacher. He writes: "The reading of this work (TLIG Messages) is for me, a priest ordained long ago in the church, a prodigious rediscovery of the Gospel and a deepening of my faith."[5] Further on he writes:

"We find in them:

"the eloquence of the prophets of the Old Testament, the serene joy of the Evangelists, the dazzling force of the Apocalypse, the wisdom of the judgements of the fathers in the desert, all within the biblical style that has the beauty of

> *the Psalms, the profound precision of the Proverbs, or the spontaneity of the Song of Songs, which will never cease to amaze me."*[6]

If these testimonies seem extravagant, there is an interesting article on the TLIG web site written by Sister H., who is a hermit nun living in Holywell, UK, titled Recognizably Jewish. She has been doing rabbinical studies for many years. Speaking of the TLIG Messages and based on Vassula's background, she writes:

> "The Holy Scriptures are quoted constantly in *True Life in God* yet without acknowledgment. They are also perfectly flowing in syntax with the rest of the text. These two aspects give a living witness to the supernatural origin of what is said. No one can make a complaint that it is a private or personal meditation because you can only meditate on what you know.
>
> "The vast quantity of Scripture quoted in sentences or phrases are beyond the mind of most people to memorize to such an extent as to quote unconsciously constantly and from all over the Scriptures and not simply from a few isolated psalms or favorite Gospel passages. Moreover, many quotations or terms are essentially Hebrew and not translated accurately in some of our modern versions of the Bible especially where the texts, if they have been looked up, would have given non-Hebraic expressions. *True Life in God* uses the correct Hebraic expressions."

Sister H. goes on to discuss nine aspects of these Messages which she considers recognizably Jewish, four of which I found particularly fascinating. She explains that grammar is not used in Biblical Hebrew and that each verse starts with 'and'. She points out that "It is rabbinical teaching that the absence of the grammar and the use of 'and' manifests that the work of God from the beginning of creation and all salvation history is one continuous unfolding act of God and is therefore expressed by one continuous sentence." In addition, in the over eleven hundred pages of the TLIG Messages there are no full stops. She claims that: "The accurate reproduction of the text, therefore, is in itself a witness of divine authorship to Jews, scripture scholars and anyone who wishes to exercise discernment when reading *True Life in God.*" It should be noted that the original printed volumes of the TLIG Messages do, indeed, have periods at the end of sentences! However, I do not think that the original handwritten version of the Messages has either stops or periods, just semicolons. Also, the newly printed, leather bound version of the Messages does not have stops or periods.

Another very interesting point that Sister H. makes is that: "The expression 'flesh and bone' in the Scriptures has an explicit meaning of kinship. We would today express kinship by saying 'you are my flesh and blood.' In the Holy Scriptures, however, that would be an abomination. All blood belongs to God; no one would dare to claim it." She says that in the Jerusalem Bible from Judges 9:2 onwards this expression is translated as 'flesh and blood.' She points out that: "*True Life in God* does not use the incorrect translation 'flesh and blood' but uses the correct Biblical expression 'the bone of My Bone, the flesh of My Flesh.' This is another example of phraseology which would have been unknown to a false prophet."

When I read the phrase "Hear My Footsteps" in the TLIG Messages, I did not understand what these words meant. Sister H. points out that this phrase "is a peculiarly Jewish expression" which "arises in connection with the fifteen signs which the Talmud sees as preceding the coming of the Messiah and the Messianic Age. The recognition of these (and Christians also have many of them in the signs to precede the Second Coming) is what Christians would call the 'Signs of the Times'. Without knowledge of Jewish phraseology a false prophet would not have used this particular Jewish phrase but would have used the Christian one of 'Signs of the Times' exclusively."

In connection with the Second Coming, Sister H. points out that the August 25, 1988 message reads: "'the first birthpangs have started but like Folly My creations laugh it off – rejecting My first signs.' The expression of the 'birthpangs' is also peculiar to Jewish expectancy of the Messiah. The 'Birthpangs of the Messiah' are used in the same way as the 'Footsteps of the Messiah;' that is, the recognizable fifteen signs preceding His Coming which are linked in the Talmud."

Obviously, Sister H. feels that with Vassula's lack of religious background, she would not be able to produce such a document of over eleven hundred pages, without introducing the types of errors Sister H. discusses in her article, Recognizably Jewish.

A similar argument has been made by Fr. James Fannan, except that the subject he is addressing relates to the theological topics covered in these Messages. Vassula had first gone to see Father James for guidance in Bangladesh, where she was living when these supernatural events began. Father James's initial reaction to Vassula was "It is satanic, diabolical…You are experiencing satanic manifestations, period!"[7]

However, sometime later Fr. James' opinion changed and he is now a solid supporter. In an interview cited by Jacques Neirynck in his book, *The Vassula Enigma*, he asked Vassula why Father James had come to believe in the Messages. Vassula responded: "What struck him was that there were no theological errors, since they had been written by someone like me, who had never studied theology, not even the catechism. He explained to me that a theological text is like a mine-field. *It is only someone who knows where the mines are who will not step on them. Theology is like that. It is touchy.*" (emphasis mine)[8] So it is also Vassula's background that serves to influence Father James' opinion of Vassula.

There are a number of sources where information can be obtained about Vassula's background and how her life changed after she got to know and love her angel, Daniel. In the past I read three of these sources, which include the *Vassula Enigma*, mentioned above, *Vassula of the Sacred Heart's Passion* by Fr. Michael O'Carroll, C.S.S.p. and Vassula's own book, *My Angel Daniel.*

Vassula was born into a Greek Orthodox family on Jan. 18, 1942 in Heliopolis, on the outskirts of Cairo, Egypt. She was surrounded by grandparents, aunts, uncles and cousins on both sides of her family who all attended a family gathering every Sunday. She went to an English school close to her home. She was an average student, weakest in mathematics. But painting was her big passion at that time and she indicates that her family was also into art. She attended classes in the Leonardo da Vinci art school in Cairo for two years.

Then suddenly, her life changed. In 1958, when Nasser nationalized all foreign firms, Vassula's father, who was an architectural engineer, was let go from his employment. They considered moving to Greece, but decided that they didn't know enough of the Greek language, particularly writing. Being more conversant in French and English, and because her mother wanted to move to a neutral country, they settled upon Switzerland. In order to master French, Vassula attended the College du Belvedere, near Chauderon. Then she took courses in secretarial work, receiving a diploma in three years, after which she got a job as an executive secretary. She worked for five years at the Bonnard store in Lausanne, now called 'Le Bon Genie.'

She married and moved to Sierra Leone with her husband who worked for the United Nations. They later moved to Sudan where her oldest son was born. Her second son was born in Ethiopia. Then the family moved to Mozambique. Sometime later, Vassula moved to Sweden where she divorced. Subsequently, she married her current husband, a Swedish international development expert, in a civil ceremony.

Although Vassula does not fall under the jurisdiction of the Congregation for the Doctrine of the Faith of the Roman Church, she has been in contact with that office. On June 26, 2002, she submitted her responses to five questions put to her by that body. In the latest books containing the TLIG Messages, Vassula is now including these questions and her answers thereto as requested by the then Cardinal Ratzinger. In answer to a question on her marital status Vassula responded: "I am not in favor of divorce…My divorce and civil remarriage was prior to my conversion. After my conversion under the light of the TLIG Messages I discovered that my martial situation was not regular…Having realized my mistake, I approached my church authorities in Lausanne and went through a process of having everything cleared according to Orthodox marital regulations."[9]

With regard to her religious background, Vassula indicates that in Egypt her family only went to Church at Eastertime. She was not taught to go to Church every Sunday. She says that "In our family, anyhow, my mother prays a lot, but only at home. She believes in God and is religious but always at home."[10] In the book, *The Vassula Enigma*, in response to the author's question whether she had any religious education, Vassula responded: "Not at all, not even the catechism." He then asks her if she had read anything about religion. She answered: "No. At that time I had not even read the Bible. Except at school a little because it was an Anglican school. We sometimes read the Psalms and learned them by heart. But I did not get any basic religious education."[11] Until 1985, except for social reasons such as marriages and funerals, Vassula rarely went to Church.

Vassula Ryden is a woman of accomplishment. Because of her upbringing and her international travels, she speaks Greek, Arabic, French, Swedish, English and some Spanish. She continued with her artistic interests and had many exhibitions of her paintings. Vassula is athletically inclined and took part in national tennis tournaments in Bangladesh. As a hobby, she took part in a number of fashion shows. She also played social bridge for seventeen years in Africa. She describes her life prior to her spectacular conversion as follows: "We always met at the club, life was easy because expatriates are well paid. We had servants, chauffeurs, guards. I had five employees at my disposal."[12]

Vassula took her artwork seriously, and was in the process of having an exhibition of her paintings. The private showing had just taken place at the Sheraton Hotel in Bangladesh. Then, on Nov. 28, 1985, at about 11am, as she was preparing a 'to do' list for a cocktail party she was holding that evening, the not only unexpected, but the unbelievable happens! This woman who never went to Church except for social occasions, who had no interest in God, who was happy and contented in her expatriate's lifestyle, surrounded by her husband, her children and her friends suddenly has an extraordinary experience. Her angel Daniel, comes to her and moves her hand as she is writing her to do list. To her amazement, she found herself writing: "I am your guardian angel and my name is Daniel."[13] Thus began one of the most delightful and awesome set of happenings I have ever heard about!

FIFTEEN

GOD'S LOVE HYMN

One of the fascinating aspects of Vassula's story is the way God sends her guardian angel, Daniel, to prepare Vassula for the Lord's coming and for the mission God has chosen for her. Vassula's initial reaction when her angel used her hand to write the words 'I am your angel Daniel' was one of delight. She immediately told her husband of this happening and showed him the piece of paper with Daniel's writing on it. According to Vassula: "He smiled, because he always keeps both feet on the ground. And he told me: 'But it's fantastic! Let me read!' He never doubted me to the point of saying: 'My wife has lost her mind.'"[1] She also told her tennis friends: "'Do you know what is happening to me? My guardian angel approaches me and talks to me.' And those girls, who were living in the same ignorance and the same whirl of activities as I, believed me right away. They were even telling me: 'Vassula, if we didn't know you we would think you were crazy.'"[2]

Vassula goes on to say that "The next day, my angel came back in the same way. I spent endless hours in a state of joy, communicating with him. The following day he came back again but, to my great surprise, he brought with him a multitude of angels from the different choirs...By the manner of their rejoicing I understood that all Heaven was feeling festive. Then, altogether, with one voice the angels sang: 'A blessed event is about to take place!'"[3] Vassula says that she felt that this event concerned her, but, although she thought about it, she couldn't figure out what it was about.

In the book, *The Vassula Enigma*, by Jacques Neirynck, Vassula tells him that the first words her angel Daniel spoke to her about God were the words: "God is near you and He loves you."[4] She goes on to say: "I must have deeply wounded the Lord at that time because the angel's words didn't have the slightest effect on me…I didn't answer and my angel didn't add anything…It was only a few days later that my guardian angel suddenly changed his attitude towards me and I noticed how grave his expression had become. In a very solemn voicc hc asked me to read the Word. *I pretended* I didn't know what 'the Word' signifies and asked him what he meant. At that point my angel looked even more serious and told me that I knew perfectly well what he meant; however, he explained that it meant the Holy Bible."[5](italics mine)

She continued to argue with her angel, telling him that it wasn't possible to buy a Holy Bible in a Muslim country like Bangladesh. Her angel responded that she could go to the American school, which her son attended, and borrow a Bible from the Library. Previously, Vassula had no reservations about telling her husband and her friends about her communication with her guardian angel, Daniel. To her, at that time, the experience was something of a lark! Angels were the *in thing* at the time. There was a very popular TV show about angels, there were numerous books about angels, and it seemed that there were pictures of angels everywhere.

But now her angel was getting serious. And taking religion seriously was obviously a source of embarrassment for Vassula. She says: "I was debating whether to go or simply stay at home and refuse. The other thing that was embarrassing me was how would my husband and all my friends react to all this. I simply could not see myself standing in front of them with a Bible! Already I was thinking of places in the house where I would hide it, were I to bring one home."[6] However, she finally did what her angel had asked her, first getting a Bible from the American school; and then starting to read it when she got it home. As she did her "eyes fell on the psalms: I read, but could not understand a single word. This was a sign from God, showing me how blind I was."[7] The fact that Vassula finally did go and get that Bible seems to me to be the first real step in her conversion process.

Her angel Daniel continued to teach her and guide her. She undergoes a period of purification when her angel reproaches her for her past life, particularly in how she had thrown away God's gifts. She says: "My angel told me that it was a great offence to God to deny and throw away His gifts. He made me see my sins with the eyes of God, the way God sees them and not the way we see them. They were so monstrous that I despised myself while weeping bitterly."[8] A little later on she indicates: "After this experience, that had left me shattered, our Eternal Father revealed Himself to me. I did not see Him with the eyes of my soul, as I used to see my angel, but I knew it was Him and heard Him."[9] Then God asks her to pray the Our Father to Him. When she finishes God indicated that she had prayed it too fast and that He was not pleased. She prays it slower the next time but God is still not pleased because she is moving. He asks her to pray it again. This continues all day! Vassula began to wonder if God was having her make-up for all those years that she had not been praying. Finally, in the evening, God is satisfied and says "Good" after each sentence she prays.

Vassula gives an extraordinarily beautiful description of what she felt during this experience of praying the Our Father all day. She writes: "And this is how it was with my first encounter with God. When I was praying the Our Father, to God, in the beginning I was distant, but His visit which lasted the whole day changed me because when I was saying this prayer to Him, I was enjoying His presence and the words I was telling Him took some meaning. He was so fatherly, very tender and very warm. The intonation of His voice was making me feel so much at ease, that somehow, during that day, instead of responding, 'Yes, Lord,' I found myself saying, 'Yes, Dad.' I had later on apologized to God for saying, 'Dad,' but He said that He had taken that word like a jewel. He seemed so very pleased. And that is how finally I realized that God has feelings and that He wanted me to tell Him this prayer with MY HEART."[10]

Originally, Vassula wrote down the messages she was receiving on scrapes of paper. Soon, however, she started using notebooks and numbering them under the guidance of the Holy Spirit. Day after day, the messages continue, becoming more and more profound, addressing the issues of our day as seen by God. Sometimes, God reads Vassula's mind and answers her directly before she can even ask her question. Other times, God urges her to speak. For example, on April 10, 1986 God asks Vassula: "are you going to ask Me your question?" Vassula responds "Do you feel we are ignoring You?" God responds: "yes, so beware of sleep…Heaven's morning star is soon to be seen; would not I, who am your Father and care for you not warn you? I am Yahweh, your Creator and you are all my children; – where, where do you think you will go? did you ever give it a thought? did you really believe you just came on your own? had you believed that I had left you? or that I never existed? did you really believe that My Word was all a dialect of collected Hebrew fairy tales? hear Me, My Word is alive and the Truth…My Word is to help you find Me;"[11]

As the messages continue and the depth of the many ideas contained therein, manifested more strongly the power and glory of God, Vassula becomes more and more concerned as to why God has chosen someone like her to be His prophet. As the end of her first year of dictation approaches, she becomes repeatedly discouraged. She does not feel that she could ever do what God is asking of her. She does not feel worthy of His Love. She writes in her notebook these very revealing words as to how she is responding to what is occurring to her: "For two days I felt terrible. Doubts again! Satan attacked me for two whole days. All this is beyond me, and I feel very discouraged. How can God be speaking to me? Every time He approached me, I would discard Him. My mind is reeling…How is it possible that God, can speak and conversate with me! I must be dreaming, yet I go for dictation…"[12] God attempts to console Vassula and reminds her that He loves her. But Vassula repeats: "I am discouraged."[13] God responds that the devil caused her to be discouraged and that therefore, He had come to encourage her.

Surprisingly, in this particular instance, God speaks words not only of encouragement but also of rebuke, reminding Vassula of how indifferent she had been to Him in the past! He says: "I have approached you although you had no love for me; I came down to tell you of the love I have for you and to remind you that I, God, always loved you;…learn that your soul lives on, so do not harm yourselves by remaining asleep;…do not leave yourselves be drifted away by the current of dead things which lead you in arid lands where dryness prevails, for you shall die; your throats will dry from the sun which will scorch you; come to Me, come and I shall fill your cup, I will brim it over with living water sweeter than wine…and I will let you rest on My green pastures; your wearied head you will rest on Me;…I do not call only the just and the blameless, I call every son and daughter of Mine irrespective to their deeds; I, God love you in the same way; you are all from Me so abide in Me;"[14]

After three years of dictating His messages to Vassula, the Lord indicates that He wants the messages published and that Vassula is now ready to begin her public mission. What is Vassula's main mission? When I think about this question, the first thing that pops into my mind is that her main mission is to unite the Protestant, Catholic and Orthodox churches. But when I think a little bit deeper, it seems to me that it is difficult to single out one mission, she has so many. However, from a spiritual point of view, what stands out in my mind most is that Vassula tasks are to make known to all the world that God exists; that He loves everyone of us equally and unconditionally and seeks our love in return; and that He is concerned that our era has strayed so far from Him.

In one of His earliest messages in Volume 1 of TLIG, God is upset that Vassula has made a request of Him using lip service only. Vassula realizes her mistake and repeats her petition, but this time she means every word she prays. God responds: "Deliver your call to Me feeling Me, like this time. I, God, feel; I feel all! I must receive from your call, love from the depths of your soul, needing Me, loving Me, **meaning every word you say. I, God, exist, and I feel!** Any call which is lip service might as well stay buried. Lip services are calls bellowing from graves. Remember I exist and feel. I wish that all my children work, giving Me joy!" (TLIG 9-30-86) (emphasis mine)

This reference to lip service is repeated again in a very powerful message from God the Father: "Vassula lean on Me; My Hand in your hand we will proceed. O era of wretchedness how far have you gone! You have gone as far as to believe that you are able to walk without Me, you have gone as far as to believe you are worthy, you have allowed Satan to feed you his vanity; wretched beyond words, sinful and blind, do not allow yourselves to rest, be alert, do not sleep for the time is near. Grow in My Spirit – approach Me with confidence and open your hearts to receive Me. **Many of you pray but your prayers do not reach Me; learn how to pray, let Me feel you. Many prayers are spilled on earth, never reaching Me."** (TLIG 2-19-88) (emphasis mine)

Vassula responds with a question. "You mean lip service Lord?" God responds: "Yes, I mean lip service. I offered you My Word to learn and now I offer you My Message to remind you of My Ways. Come and learn – I will replace your wickedness by love. Accept My Ways, My Ways of Virtue. Era of Unfaithfulness, why have you forgotten My Divine Ways? Return to Me your Savior – I have not forsaken you and inspite of all your sins I love you. My Heart is an Abyss of Love – an Abyss of Forgiveness;" (TLIG 2-19-88)

For me, personally, these concepts that God exists, that He loves us and wants a return of love, and that He is concerned that so many people are far from Him, made a very strong impression on me. And associated with these concepts there is a sort of corollary that relates closely to all three of them. That is, the emphasis on mystical contemplation and the guidance that God gives us so that we may all reach the transforming union with the Triune God, that I found throughout the TLIG Messages. Every word that God addresses to Vassula is also meant for us. Repeatedly, the Triune God tells us that He thirsts for our love. That He thirsts for all the lost souls.

Another interesting aspect of these messages is that God is teaching Vassula step by step. It is absolutely fascinating to read the early messages and to see how God leads her. This interchange took place in 1987 when Vassula was just learning. He reminds her of her nothingness, her littleness and her wretchedness. She is undergoing another period of doubt. Vassula writes: "God Almighty, I do not want to fall into vanity or self-interest. I ask you to help me! I want to remain a nothing; I want to remain plain and give You all the glory!" God responds: "Vassula, have you forgotten how you were a year ago? My beloved, let Me remind you: when I, Yahweh, was passing among the dead [the spiritual dead], I saw you there among the wicked; they were holding you, tormenting you; I saw you lying there struggling on your own, your soul close to death; I felt full of pity for you;…for how many years I have been outside your door waiting, waiting that one day you might hear Me…Finally, you called Me; I lifted you to My Breast, daughter, and I healed your wounds; I taught you how to love Me, I taught you how to receive Me by elevating you, and I let My Light shine upon you; My flower, do not despair; I am teaching you step by step, *with the vocabulary you understand;"* (TLIG 2-12-87) (italics mine)

In discussing *lectio divina*, Abbot Thomas Keating points out that the last step, *contemplatio* or contemplation, is the "state of resting in the presence of God." (To emphasize the word 'rest' I am putting it in italics in the following paragraphs.) Over and over again, as I read the TLIG Messages I came across such words as "*rest* in Me" or "let us *rest* in each other." God's use of the word *rest* is yet another way He uses to call each of us to mystical contemplation. For example, when Vassula is talking to God and becomes concerned that maybe she is not doing enough to love Him, God responds with these amazing words: "come, do not misunderstand Me! it's Love talking, it's Love's desires, it's Love's Flame, it's Love's Jealous Love; I cannot stand rivals; lean on your Holy Father, Spouse, Companion and God; come, *let us rest in each other;* Love Me, daughter, with a jealous love too;" (TLIG 5-5-87)

There are two messages that, not only refer to *resting* in God, but also speak in precious words of His Sacred Heart. Jesus says: "My Vassula, remember you are not of this world, you belong to Me. Can you see My Sacred Heart? Enter in My Sacred Heart; in its depths you will find your *rest*;" (11-8-87) Almost ten years later, Jesus again speaks of His Sacred Heart, saying these beautiful words: "My fragile one, wander no more like a vagabond but allow Me to draw you in Me; enjoy My Presence, enjoy My great wealth of My Heart, you to whom I allied Myself by marriage; I have become your royal counselor;…come closer to your Beloved and take your shelter in His embrace, then your soul will rejoice in His embrace; no one will disturb your *rest*; no one can touch your *rest* in My Heart because I will safely guard you, My Beloved;" (TLIG 5-6-97)

In my Chapter Thirteen on Mystical Contemplation, I discussed how I believed that the only way we could live the Scriptural precept that we should "pray without ceasing" (1 Th. 5:17) is to become a contemplative. Vassula, herself, speaks frequently of what she refers to as the ***unceasing prayer***. In her talk on Repentance prepared for the True Life in God Pilgrimage in Egypt in October 2002, Vassula tells us that God is calling all of us to a life of unceasing prayer. She defines unceasing prayer as the "permanent state of contemplation and union with God." She emphasizes that it is "through repentance that we enter into the unceasing prayer." She describes the unceasing prayer in these very beautiful words: "The unceasing prayer is when we allow God to live perpetually in us and we in Him. The unceasing prayer is when our spirit is completely absorbed in God, becoming sensitive to God's presence. In these moments we do not need anymore words to express ourselves to God because all our being becomes a vivid flame. Enflamed with love for God. In these moments of this silent prayer, our spirit forgets the world and is ravished in this silence, enjoying every moment of having been captured by God."

In the first issue of the new TLIG Magazine, September 2006, Vassula writes on The Union of Divine Love in the Holy Trinity. She again speaks of the unceasing prayer: "God is urging us to follow Him and perfect our union with the Three Divine Persons, for in perfecting our union with the Holy Trinity, our thoughts, our acts, our sayings will be in total harmony with the Divine Will of God since everything will be regulated and ordered by Love. In that divine union all that belongs to the Trinity will belong to the one united with Them. When the soul has given herself up to the Will of God, the mind then contains nothing else save God, and our life will be turned into an unceasing prayer and we would stand before God with a pure mind."

Another aspect of the way that contemplative prayer is presented in the TLIG Messages, is that it often presents contemplation in terms of ***spousal mysticism.*** There are excellent examples of this in the article mentioned in the previous paragraph. For example, Vassula writes: "God is trying to stir our love and raise us all into leading a contemplative life resting in the nuptial chamber of His Heart." Vassula quotes this message as an example. Jesus says: "I will rouse their thirst to seek My Heart alone; as a king who sits on his royal throne, dressed in all his robes of state, glittering with gold and precious stones, with a scepter in his right hand; I will take it as My prime and personal concern to preserve My Throne in your heart, so that you heart will continue to be adorned with the wealth of your King and Lord; this wealth of knowing Me in My triune glory; the wealth of fearing Me and the wealth of shunning every kind of sin, and finally, the wealth of doing My Divine Will and what is pleasing to Me, your God;" (TLIG 5-6-97)

In the same article, there is an unusually beautiful quote from God. In this example there is an explicit reference to nuptial mysticism. God says: "I, Yahweh, can adorn your spirit, lavishly offering you a flow of My Divine Love so that you, in your turn return to Me this flow of Love; then, wait and see, the day I will draw you into the nuptial chamber of My Heart, like a rose that grows on the bank of a watercourse, you will blossom to declare the greatness of My Name, calling Me: 'my Father;'" (TLIG 9-25-97)

One final example of nuptial mysticism, which also highlights the fact that, in His TLIG Messages, God speaks to ***everyone in the world***, not just Christians. Also of note is how He refers to His Second Coming and to the Kingdom He will establish on earth. "I tell you solemnly, many of you who are not born of the Spirit shall receive from above by My Grace the Spirit of Truth; The Spirit of Truth shall descend in all His radiant Glory out of Heaven and make His Home in you, My Holy Spirit shall wed you to become His bride, embellishing you by His Holiness, and suddenly the Heavenly things will become visible in your hearts, and My

Kingdom unseen yet to the heart shall become visible and crystal clear in all its Glory;"(TLIG 6-2-91)

A number of recent apparitions throughout the world have apocalyptic prophecies associated with them. Vassula has also received such apocalyptic messages. In this instance, it is St. Mary, as Vassula refers to Our Lady, who gives the following message to Vassula: "Realize that these are special days you are living in your times, these are the days preceding the Lord's Coming, they are the opening of the path where the Lord will come;...<u>the world is dead to love,</u> it lies in deep obscurity because hatred, greed, and selfishness dominate the entire earth all the way to its core; I am shaken by terrible sights, with the iniquities of this dark world and the apostasy that penetrated in the sanctuary itself, the disasters, famine, afflictions, war and plague, all these are drawn by you; all that comes from the earth returns to earth; the earth is autodestructing itself and *it is not God who gives you all these disasters as many of you tend to believe;* God is Just and all Merciful, but evil draws evil; pray hard, pray with your heart for the conversion and the salvation of your era;"(TLIG 5-15-90) (italics mine)

The following message from God, the Father is a very revealing example of this apocalyptic element. Also very interesting is how He depicts the reaction of many people to Vassula and her messages. He says: "Daughter, you are in charge of My Message, and I have been sending you in the world from nation to nation to cry out repentance and reduce this wilderness – indeed, the crowds throng around you; it has come to their ear that I Am is speaking, and nation after nation is talking about you; they say to each other: 'Let us go and hear what God is saying.' They come in thousands and sit down in front of you and listen to your words, but who acts on them? As far as they are concerned, you are like a love song beautifully sung to music; your words enchant them, but who among them puts My Messages into practice? Have they understood the words: reconciliation, peace, love and unity? When brimstone and devouring flames will take place, and they are very near you now, they will learn that I had sent a prophet among them." (TLIG 12-13-92)

In contrast to this message, in the TLIG magazine of September 2006 in an article titled The Real Message of True Life in God, Vassula says that her messages are not messages "of doom and gloom." She reminds those who concentrate on catastrophes and disasters and are living under fear of such happenings, that "God might surprise you, and you in your turn might feel very disappointed, just like Jonah about Nineveh." In the messages, the ***Second Coming*** is mentioned as well as the ***End of Times.*** Vassula points out that the End of Times does not mean the end of the world, but rather the end of an epoch! There are numerous references to Scripture in the TLIG Messages concerning the Book of Daniel and the Book of Revelations, as well as other books of the Bible that refer to this Second Coming.

One reference to the Book of Revelations that I found particularly enlightening, refers to the Sacred Heart of Jesus and the Immaculate Heart of Mary. I must admit that I never had a particular devotion to the Sacred Heart. I did not understand the emphasis on this mystery. It seemed somewhat sentimental to me! I got a whole new insight into this devotion in reading an article by Robert Carroll, titled The *Blossoming* of the Sacred Heart of Jesus in True Life in God which I found on the TLIG web site. In this article, the writings of Father Michael O'Carroll are discussed relative to his special devotion to the Sacred Heart of Jesus. He is an author and spiritual advisor to Vassula, and has written more than 20 books on Marian theology, hagiography and the Papacy, as well as five theological encyclopedias.

Speaking of what Father Michael O'Carroll has to say about the origins of the concept of the Sacred Heart, the author of the article, Robert Carroll writes: "Father Michael O'Carroll tells us that although it was not until the Thirteenth

Century revelation to St. Gertrude that the Sacred Heart is first mentioned, we were indeed being prepared for the Inexhaustible Treasure even before the birth of Christ. 'There were three great civilizations around the ancient Mediterranean basin: the Roman, based on law; the Greek, based on the intellect and exemplified by Aristotle and Plato, among others; and the Jewish civilization, based on the heart and exemplified in the writings of the Old Testament wherein there are 850 references to the heart as expressing the whole person in response to the problems of life. We see this again and again in the tender, intimate language of the Psalms. Jesus, the manifestation of the divine heart, took from the Old Testament when he said, "Blessed are the pure of heart, for they shall see God." St. Thomas Aquinas taught that this beatitude summarizes the entire Gospel of Jesus Christ.'"

When I studied the Book of Revelation using the Little Rock Scripture program, the commentary related the subjects contained therein to the reactions of the early Church to the happenings of that time. There was no mention of the Book of Revelation predicting future events! This interpretation seemed to me to be just that, an interpretation; and I just didn't buy it. I felt that the Book of Revelation did refer to the future, probably the end of time. And I often wondered about Jesus' words: "I have come to set fire to the earth, and how I wish it were already kindled!" (Luke 12:49) How does one interpret such enigmatic words? For some reason I thought this statement was related to the book of Revelations, but I didn't know how. Neither could I understand the symbology or meaning of the text in the Book of Revelation. That is, not until I read the TLIG Messages regarding the Book of Apocalypse, the Book of Daniel and other Scripture references to the Second Coming; and heard Vassula's insights on certain messages she had received.

For example, here is one of the messages given to Vassula relative to the meaning of some of the symbology in the books of Revelation and Zechariah. The Sacred Hearts of Jesus and Mary are identified as the 'two witnesses' who have been appointed to prophesy and who are represented in Scripture by Elijah and Moses. The Sacred Heart of Jesus and the Immaculate Heart of Mary are also the two anointed ones symbolized by the 'two lamps,' the 'two olive trees' and the 'two olive branches.' Christ informs us that He has been giving all of us "signs of the Times," of which the reference to the two witnesses is an example. Here are some of His words: "some will ask 'where are Elijah and Moses who are to come?' I tell you, you evil generation: We [The two hearts of Jesus and Mary] have not been speaking parables all these years; Elijah and Moses have come already and you have not recognized them but treated them as you pleased;...Our Two Hearts have not been speaking to you in parables nor in riddles; all our Words were Light and Our Hearts like Two Lamps are shining near each other, so bright, that everyone may see, but you have not understood;...Our Two Hearts are anointed [Zc. 4:14] and are living, They are like a sharp sword, double-edged [Ap. 1:16] prophesying, but the rebellious spirit in this generation is re-crucifying My Word [Allusion to Ap. 11:8-10] the double-edged sword, and are rejecting Our Two Hearts who speak to you today;" (TLIG 12-24-91)

For me, the TLIG Messages are summed up in the 'Greatest commandment,' that is that we love God with all our hearts, and that we love our neighbor as God loves him. And the only way that I see this as being even remotely possible, is that we live in a state of continuous union with God. Then, it is Jesus in me, who loves everyone. And as I am united with Jesus I am also united with everyone in the world. And thus Jesus' priestly prayer to the Father that "All may be one" is fulfilled. Over and over again in the TLIG Messages, God stresses that He wants His churches to unite and that He is sending Vassula to announce this fact to the world. In just one of the many different messages on

Christian unity, Jesus directs Vassula: "My Vassula, draw three iron bars with a head on the top, these represent the Roman Catholics, the Orthodox and the Protestants. I want them to bend and unite but these iron bars are stiff and cannot bend on their own, so <u>I shall have to come to them with My Fire and with the power of My Flame upon them they shall turn soft to bend and mold into one solid iron bar, and My Glory will fill the whole earth.</u>" (TLIG 10-26-89)

This theme of church unity, is presented in yet another way by Our Lord to Vassula on Oct. 7, 1991. He tells her that she must carry His cross of unity! These are His words: "Daughter, for My sake, take My Cross of Unity and carry it across the world. Go from country to country and tell those who speak of unity, yet never cease to think the contrary and continue to live the contrary, that <u>their division has separated My Heart from theirs</u>;" (TLIG 10-7-91) On another occasion, speaking again of unity, Jesus laments: "I observe every action from Heaven, and I know that the most impressive wounds I will receive would be in the house of My best friends. I will have to drink of the Cup of your division, your unreconciled heart and of your apostasy;" (TLIG 4-16-93)

When I first read that God, not only wants all the Christian churches to unite, but rather that Jesus had said to Vassula that: "I Am, I, Jesus <u>guarantee</u> to you all that My Church will be one, united;" (TLIG 11-30-87), I wondered. It was difficult for me to even conceive of the possibility that such a thing would ever happen in this modern day world of ours. However, I now see it quite differently. I am thoroughly convinced that it will happen! If not in my lifetime, certainly within the next generation. That is just an example of how my faith in what these messages foretold grew as I read them again and again.

And as my belief in the messages grew, so did its fruits. First, and foremost was the emphasis that God is inviting all of us to a life of mystical contemplation. The mystical path that God was leading me along was a very quiet and unspectacular one, not filled with the mystical phenomena and constant assurances of God's love, that graced Vassula's life for so many years. However, the messages filled me with a love of God and repeated assurances that I should continue the path that I was following no matter how difficult it seemed at times.

Secondly, I was somewhat disillusioned after Vatican II, when there were so many changes in the Catholic Church that I became uncertain as to what was and was not required of a catholic. My loyalty to the Holy See was shaken. A major effect of reading not only Vassula's messages but also Gianna Sullivan's messages, was that my confidence in, and sense of obedience to Peter's chair was greatly increased. Thirdly, I always had a problem in fully appreciating Holy Scripture, although I studied it with a Baptist, and was a Little Rock Bible Study facilitator. Reading the TLIG Messages has changed all that. Now when I go to daily Mass I look forward eagerly to the Liturgy of the Word, because the passages from both the Old and the New Testaments now have a new and potent meaning for me!

Over the years since I first heard about Vassula, I have followed her path carefully. I bought all her books as soon as I was aware that they were available. I took various members of my family and friends to at least five of her presentations, the last one was in October 2006 in Ottawa, Canada. I read her newsletter regularly and just subscribed to her new TLIG magazine, the first issue of which was published in September 2006. The reason that I mention how I have followed Vassula all these years, is to make it clear how seriously I took the TLIG Messages and how I followed the progress of Vassula's mission. In a letter dated Dec. 31, 2001 Vassula wrote: "Since two years now I had been urging every reader of TLIG, [and you are many] to become a witness. This year though it was evident that Our Lord was pushing me to push you. Why? Because he saw that some of you were ready to go out and evangelize and christianize this dechristanized society!" When I read Vassula's words I felt I had to do something, but I didn't know what it should be. So I prayed for guidance and discernment to know God's will.

At first I thought that maybe God wanted me to start a TLIG prayer group in my home. However, I had already been thinking that God wanted me to do something on the World Wide Web, but I didn't know what. As I describe in my chapter, The Invisible Wall, I finally decided that God wanted me to direct my efforts toward promoting the *Lessons from Our Lord* that the visionary, Gianna Sullivan, had received; as well as to promote a JESUS of MERCY Contemplative Prayer Group, real-time on the internet; and to write this book, *Its Light is the Lamb, An Unexpected Spiritual Journey.* The interesting fact is that this decision to help promote the triumph of Mary's Immaculate Heart in Emmitsburg, MD was made at the promptings of Vassula to become a witness! Of course, she was talking about TLIG! But I am, in fact, witnessing for the TLIG mission in this book of mine, as well as in my personal witnessing to friends and acquaintances.

SIXTEEN

OUR LADY OF EMMITSBURG

In Chapter Six, when we left the visionary, Dr. Gianna Talone-Sullivan, in Scottsdale, AZ, she had just married Dr. Michael Sullivan. On Nov. 1, 1993, at the request of Our Lady, the newlyweds moved to Emmitsburg, MD. They were warmly welcomed by Fr. Al Pehrrson, a Vincentian priest, and pastor of St. Joseph's Church in Emmitsburg, MD. Gianna and Michael had visited Fr. Al earlier in the year, after being directed to see him by Our Lady who appeared to Gianna in the Grotto of Lourdes, Emmitsburg, MD. Our Lady told Gianna to tell Fr. Al what had occurred in the Grotto and how Our Lady had invited them to move to Emmitsburg.

Dom Forker, in his book *Our Lady of Emmitsburg*, asked Fr. Al how he felt about this very unusual situation and whether he ever had any doubts about Gianna's authenticity? Fr. Al responded: "Yes, at one time, I had prudent doubts. But Fr. Jack Spaulding dispelled most of those. Then she won my confidence that first Wednesday night, on Nov. 3, 1993, at the Marian Prayer Group devotion in the Community House. First, Our Lady addressed my two secret concerns. But second, Gianna addressed the promise I had made to God six years before. Only I, in my heart, knew what it was. Our Lady had to tell her. That was enough for me. I knew she was legitimate." [1]

The Wednesday night to which Fr. Pehrrson refers, Nov. 3, 1993, was the first time that Gianna Sullivan and her husband attended the Marian Prayer Group conducted by two Sisters of Charity in the Chapel in St. Vincent's Community House. As the third decade of the rosary was being prayed Gianna went into ecstasy when Our Lady appeared to her. That night Our Lady of Emmitsburg gave Gianna her first public message under that title for the world. Following that first Wednesday night, Our Lady continued giving public messages to Gianna for the world each Wednesday (later changed to Thursday) until Sept. 7, 2000.

When Mike and Gianna moved to Emmitsburg in 1993, he had just finished phasing out his medical practice in Phillipsburg, Pa. In the previous year, the Lord had asked Gianna to restore dignity to mankind through love, but He left the details up to Gianna. Considering that Mike was a physician and that she had a doctorate in pharmacology and a background in insurance, Gianna thought that there must be some way of their helping to provide for the medical needs of the poor and homeless. She finally decided on a large recreational vehicle that she and Mike converted to a medical van and took it to areas where the needy could easily access their van. That was the beginning of the Mission of Mercy which provides free health care to the uninsured working poor and the homeless.

The Mission of Mercy personnel try to treat each patient with respect for their humaneness, with dignity and with love. In the book, *Our Lady of Emmitsburg* by Dom Forker, Gianna is quoted as saying: "Christ on the cross was the epitome of all forms of humiliation...The poor and the underprivileged, through no fault of their own, are treated in a way that accentuates humiliation, especially the people that we see. They don't look very good. In fact, they don't smell very good. Their dignity has been stripped away from them, and we as a society strip it even further. We continue to humiliate them and add to their self-mortification."[2]

The Mission of Mercy has continued to grow over the years and is now located in three states, Maryland,

Pennsylvania and Arizona. The first Arizona site was opened in October 1997. According to Gianna, "Our Lord and Our Lady directed us to go there."[3] There are now four clinics in Arizona, two in Pennsylvania and seven in Maryland. They not only provide free medical care and medicines, but also free dental care in seven of the clinics. There currently are 282 active volunteers in the Maryland and Pennsylvania clinics. According to Dom Forker, Gianna has said that "Our Lord and Our Lady told her that she and the Mission of Mercy would be *kept hidden* and saved for the last."[4]

I had no idea that Gianna had moved east and was having apparitions weekly in St. Joseph's Church in Emmitsburg. However, Mimi Jaye, one of the women in our bible study and a very devout charismatic catholic, had heard about Gianna's presence in Emmitsburg. When she told me about it, I was delighted, particularly since Gianna had not been present the time that my sister and I had flown to Scottsdale, AZ. to St. Maria Goretti Church to attend the Thursday night prayer meeting there. I immediately made plans to drive to Emmitsburg, MD. Since, no one I knew seemed interested in going, I went by myself.

Mimi Jaye had told me of the fact that the secretary at St. Joseph's Church in Emmitsburg saved some seats in the Church for those who had to drive a long distance to get to Emmitsburg. So I called the secretary and she promised to save me a seat and told me to meet her at St. Joseph's rectory at a certain time. When I arrived at the rectory, a number of people were already there waiting. The secretary took us as a group across the road to the side of the Church. Just as we finished crossing the road, the secretary turned to us and asked if we had smelled the roses? She told us that it happens frequently and that it was particularly strong just as we stepped into the street from the rectory side. We retraced our path and as we did, the fragrance of roses was quite apparent to us! There were no roses to be seen but nonetheless the scent was there. And as I walked back across the road and along the side of the Church, I continued to smell the roses. It stopped when I entered St. Joseph's Church. However, later in the church when we were praying the rosary, I once again noted the scent of roses for a few moments.

As we were walking beside the Church, I wondered to myself if our group had responded to the power of suggestion, and perhaps we had just imagined that we smelled the roses. I also thought that maybe someone in the group had a strong perfume that smelled like roses. I looked about me carefully to see if there was possibly something that we had missed that was the source of the scent. But I didn't see anything. The fact that I smelled the roses again, but only for a few moments inside the Church, seemed to belie the possibilities I had considered. Another interesting aspect of all this was that after I returned home to New Hyde Park, I again smelled the scent of roses three separate times when I was attending services in Notre Dame Church. I had never before smelled roses that I couldn't see or for which there was no apparent source, nor has it ever happened since these five instances which I just cited.

Considering, that for most of my adult life, I had not been particularly attracted to private revelations, it is hardly surprising that I had even less interest in allegedly supernatural happenings, that related mostly to inanimate objects. When I heard of such things as holy statues weeping, people getting the scent of roses when no roses were present or even Sacred Hosts bleeding, I paid little attention to these reports, except that I felt a little uncomfortable when it came to Sacred Hosts bleeding. And I certainly was not expecting that I would smell the scent of roses when I went to the Marian Prayer meeting in Emmitsburg. What surprised me was not the fact that I had smelled roses but rather, how I reacted. I was pleased that I had smelled the non existent roses!!! When I thought about it much later, I realized that for me to feel that way, was surely an indication that I was finally beginning to learn to be *little*!

Speaking of littleness, in His Lessons Jesus emphasizes how important He considers this attitude: "I desire to teach them now and encourage them to be *little* children, little in all ways; actions, thoughts, deeds and speech; little through simplicity and humility of heart." Lest we think that He is promoting a sort of namby-pamby attitude, Christ makes it quite clear that this is not the case. Littleness does not mean that we let people walk all over us. Christ continues: "Do not mistake littleness with lack of power. Littleness is detachment from possessions and is purity of heart. It is simpleness and the wisdom to avoid the influence of wickedness. Littleness is not associated with lack of wealth, prestige or success."[5]

When Our Lord and Our Lady speak to the visionaries of our time they often use the words *little* or *child*. For example, Jesus says to Vassula: "Come now, little friend, do not stop loving Me." (TLIG 4-8-91) Or again: "Little one do not get discouraged in this exile." (TLIG 7-16-91) Or in the *I am your JESUS of MERCY* books, Jesus frequently uses the words "My dear child" or "My child" to Gianna. And Our Lady addresses Gianna in the plural, saying "My dear little children." I wondered at this frequent use of the diminutive. After thinking about it on and off for a while, I began to postulate that one reason was the fact that God wants to teach me and others like me that we have to be child-like in accepting these supernatural happenings. In other words, I have to be just like a child who places its faith and trust in loving parents. That isn't always so easy. In the past, it would have bothered me, particularly as I would start to imagine people smiling at my apparent simplicity in accepting that Jesus is speaking and teaching us in these modern times!

Interestingly, in the Lessons Jesus anticipates this criticism. He says to Gianna that those who think that He would not "speak in so pedestrian a way" are fooling themselves. They are letting the complexity of their intellects control them! He quotes such people as saying: "Jesus is all knowing with great intellect, and could not or would not speak simply."[6] God emphasizes, over and over again, to the visionaries of whom I am writing, that we cannot know Him through the intellect. Rather, it is through the heart that we come to know Him. This, in essence, is the way of the mystic! Again, in another message Jesus gives us an insight into His words about complexity. He says, at a Thursday Night Prayer meeting in Scottsdale, AZ: "I want to say to you this night, 'My way is simple!' My dear ones, you cause yourselves much pain when you complicate My way."[7]

This concept, that we cause ourselves much unnecessary pain when we do not put into practice what the Holy Spirit is telling us through His prophets, is another interesting aspect of these messages. The corollary to this is the tremendous amount of pain that we inflict on each other without our being fully aware of the implications of our daily actions in all this. These are two very important lessons for me. I have difficulty appreciating how complicated I frequently make my spiritual journey! I am often bothered by all the ***shoulds*** and ***oughts*** that weigh me down, as I forget how by abandoning myself to God, seeking only to know and do His Will, these pressures are taken away.

Over and over again, these messages stress that what Jesus asks of us is to ***focus*** on Him, and even more strongly to ***be*** Him! And, of course, the only way of truly ***being*** Jesus is to be united with Him in mystical contemplation! As I have said earlier, one of the most important things to me about the Lessons from Jesus, is their emphasis on contemplative prayer. Just as He does in the True Life in God messages to Vassula Ryden, in one of His Lessons to Gianna Sullivan, Jesus invites us (all His people), in very beautiful and consoling words, that are also simple and uncomplicated, to come before Him in the Blessed Sacrament and rest in His Sacred Heart:

"Put aside all distractions, fear, worry and concern. Realize you are before Me and contemplate My love and goodness. If you will absorb My love and rest in My love, your heart, mind and soul ***will be rejuvenated and will rise to an ecstasy of joy***. When you rest in My Heart, a peace overcomes you, almost a state of sleep; but you are resting truly in My Most Sacred Heart where I am carrying you and sifting through all your needs and organizing all your spiritual and temporal needs for the glory of God the Father."[8](italics mine)

The second important lesson for me is that I have gained a deeper insight into how much suffering I, myself, cause others. I thought that I had no responsibility for all the wars and fighting, nor for the shortage of resources all over the world. But, if I look honestly into my soul, I realize that I am responsible for all these things. As Jesus tells me: "It is dangerous to blame others for war. It is dangerous to blame others for lack of resources. It is dangerous to blame others for lack of health. First, you must look to yourself and see your own lack of love….It is lack of love of which you yourself are guilty that has led to wars, crime, lack of resources, hunger and pain."[9] When I think about these words it becomes clearer to me that it is my selfishness that Jesus is talking about. He is telling me that I must try to love unconditionally since such love cannot coexist with selfishness. But how do I love everyone unconditionally? It isn't possible! Yet, in her first message to Gianna Sullivan in November 1993 Our Lady of Emmitsburg says that it is possible to love unconditionally and she tells us how: "Strive always to abandon yourself unconditionally to God, so that you will be able to love unconditionally."[10]

In another Lesson, Jesus gave me a profound insight into how He views us despite our often grievous failings. He describes different types of people and what motivates them and says to take note because “they are all good, yet lost.” He speaks of people who “are full of remorse, guilt and low self acceptance” and who realize that they do not merit Heaven. Then there are people who are “apprehensive and overly cautious” who are controlled by their intellect and do not trust their hearts. Jesus speaks of His “doubting Thomases who wonder if My lessons are truly from Me.” Then there are His confident people, “those who make their time table. But I am at the end of their list!” And finally there are people whom “money has enticed to the point where it becomes their god. My people of materialism!”[11] Jesus continues by repeating the somewhat surprising statement that: “They are all good.” What struck me is how consistent this statement is with the commonly accepted idea, that we are all basically good. However, Jesus does add a ‘but.’ He says that they “need the grace of my salvation.” He concludes with a very sobering statement: “Those who fall into the trap of evil, can be saved through prayer and devotion. However, those who turn away by their own free will from the Trinity, lose life forever!”[12]

One of the things that I like so much about these messages, and that was personally consoling to me, is the fact that Jesus teaches us in these Lessons to recognize and accept our sinfulness as we progress on our spiritual journey. He tells us that we must accept ourselves with love! He describes in beautiful language what happens as we choose to walk with Him each day. Jesus says: “The ego slowly dwindles away and disintegrates, and My people will even accept and acknowledge their human faults. Then they will no longer walk in false humility but be the budding beauties of humbleness!” He encourages us by saying that when we try to do what is right and fail, that we actually have won in His sight! And He adds: “I am not looking for perfectionism, but genuine sensitivity."[13] In my naiveté, I thought that God expected us to ultimately reach perfection in this life! His understanding of our humaneness is very evident in these words: "You can be merciful. You can be loving. You can **be Me**, for you were created in My goodness. It takes time to utilize and put into practice My words, as it takes time for an athlete to train and rise to a level of perfection in fitness. If you do not start, how will you reach the finish line? Begin now and be patient with yourself."[14]

Just as there are apocalyptic messages associated with the True Life in God Messages of Vassula Ryden, there are also such prophecies contained in the Lessons from Jesus as well as in some of the other messages Gianna has received. And like Vassula, Gianna says she is not a messenger of "gloom and doom." In the book, *Our Lady of Emmitsburg*, Gianna is quoted as saying: "What makes me different from the other visionaries is that I'm not 'doom and gloom'...My symbols are love and mercy...The Blessed Mother calls Emmitsburg the 'Center of Her Immaculate Heart.' The 'Center of Love and Mercy.'"[15]

Relative to some of the prophecies and warnings mentioned in these messages, it is interesting to consider one of the earliest Lessons. As I reread this passage, I realize that God was talking about one of my particular problems, that is, that I had my own definition of God and of how He should act. I tried to do everything myself because I did not really understand what God's grace was all about! In this Lesson on MERCY Jesus laments: "My people will not let Me be their God! They make Me out to be Who they think I should be. How much longer do you think this can continue before man corrupts the gift of this world totally? **Man expects to accomplish on his own.** The pain I feel is because the beauty of this world was once given as a symbol of the love of God."[16] (emphasis mine)

In another Lesson Jesus continues on this theme of how beautiful the world once was, and adds a new subject, how short time is getting. And He returns to this theme of how time is now running out for us, quite a number of times. Jesus says: "**My dear one, the time of My mercy is at hand. I simply am asking for love, respect and mercy on one another.** Is that too much to request from a God, who constructed a world of beauty for His people; who were constructed in His likeness and His beauty? You say 'no', but look around you and observe My people, who say they love. The world was so beautiful, but My people have made it so ugly. There is hope to recapture My beauty…but, little time to do so."[17]

Jesus relates this emphasis on lack of time to His Second Coming. There is a warning to us, implicit in his words, that if we do not take action now, if the apocalyptic predictions of disaster take place, we will not be able to decide for God at that time. The Lessons and messages keep pointing out to us that one does not change overnight. That it takes time for us human beings to go through the necessary steps! For example, Jesus warns us in an enigmatic message, that: "When I come, it will be during a time of standard, day-to-day functioning. But I tell you...it will be too late to come back! COME BACK TO ME NOW!"[18]

Even though this message sounds very threatening, I agree fully with Gianna that, taken as a whole, these are not messages of 'doom and gloom.' The allegedly apocalyptical messages that seem to predict doom are few in comparison to all the messages that have been received by Gianna from God the Father, from Jesus and from Our Lady. One has to read the complete set, at least of the Lessons from Jesus and the messages of God the Father to fully understand the context in which things are said and/or to read all of what Our Lady has said. For example, in one of her messages, Our Lady of Emmitsburg places a different emphasis on the Second Coming. Rather than warning us of coming danger,

Mary speaks of "hope and joy." Our Lady says: "I desire you, little children, to have the anticipation of Jesus' coming with hope and joy. He is your Savior and He will save you if you will allow Him. He is coming to gather His lost sheep for He does not desire one to go astray. Have hope in Jesus and rejoice, for He is coming to rescue you from the snares of the evil one, and His mercy is endless."[19]

A fascinating insight into the Second Coming is that, according to Gianna, Jesus is coming as the ***Child*** Jesus! This is perhaps the most controversial aspect of her messages. On March 2, 2000, Our Lady of Emmitsburg told Gianna that: "Jesus will come a Second Time and reign. He is coming, and it will be the return of Jesus as a Child to enlighten the minds and hearts of all people, of all faiths, of all nations and of every race. His Kingdom shall be an era of peace and hope, and it will be a spiritual quenching for your parched souls." To me, this seems to be an obviously spiritual message. Note how Our Lady refers to a "spiritual quenching" for our "parched souls." But many have believed that this message meant that Jesus would come again, walk this earth, and perhaps, actually reign over a material kingdom. Our Lady makes it quite clear what she means on June 29, 2000 when she says that this is not a new or novel theology. The Mother of God says:

> "I have told you that this is my Son, the Child Jesus, who will return again, ***not*** in a corporeal body to walk the earth, and ***not*** as the glorified Just Judge as He will come at the end of time, but as a Child of Hope to usher in an era of peace as God's Mercy is unveiled. This has been foretold for many centuries and is ***not*** a new theology which many seem to believe."

It appears that the apocalyptic tone in some of the messages was brought to the attention of certain officials of the Diocese of Baltimore, MD, of which St. Joseph's Church in Emmitsburg is part, because shortly thereafter a commission was established by Cardinal William H. Keeler to study Gianna's mystical experiences. On September 8, 2000, Gianna and Mike received notification from Archbishop Keeler's office that they were suspending the Marian Prayer Meetings at St. Joseph's Church in Emmitsburg, pending this evaluation. One of the saddest aspects of this notification was that it came on the feast of Our Lady! Gianna accepted this notification with grace and said to her followers: "This is a gift. Be at peace." (Website Background by Dom Forker) It would seem that not only were Gianna and Mike submitting with obedience to Church directions, but the Mother of God also accepted this directive! For two years, Our Lady did not give any new public messages to Gianna for the world, although she continued to appear to Gianna almost daily.

On Aug. 5, 2002, Our Lady resumed her public messages to Gianna for the world. And, in September 2002, Cardinal Keeler sent a letter to Fr. William O'Brien, CM, pastor of St. Joseph's parish and apparently indicated that they were continuing their ban on the use of catholic facilities in the archdiocese by Dr. Gianna Sullivan for dissemination of her messages. The report of the commission has not been made public. However, Msgr. Jeremiah F. Kenney, Cardinal Keeler's Delegate for Canonical Affairs sent a brief communication to Dr. Gianna Talone-Sullivan on Sept. 24, 2002. In the Frederick News-Post of Sunday, December 8, 2002, Gianna's husband, Dr. Michael Sullivan, is quoted as saying: "the church only restricted using the church property to deliver the messages and the Commission did not specifically condemn or approve the messages." During those two years and continuing to this day, a number of well known catholic priests have voiced their strong support for Dr. Gianna Sullivan. For example, the Rev. John B. Wang, Ph. D., J. U. D. is quoted in the same article as saying that he personally believes that "Gianna is a chosen soul of Our

Lord." More testimonies can be found on the web site of the Foundation of the Sorrowful and Immaculate Heart of Mary in Emmitsburg, MD.

However, in 2001 the Foundation and its web site had not been created and hence I had no idea of what had happened on September 8, 2000. When I began thinking about possibly putting the Lessons from Our Lord on my planned web site I decided to get in touch with Gianna to ask her permission. However, when I called the Rectory of St. Joseph's Church to ask them how to get in touch with Gianna, I learned that the prayer meetings in St. Joseph's Church had been discontinued. When I asked the secretary at the Rectory how to contact Gianna she said she could not help me. I therefore decided to make a trip to Emmitsburg to see if there was some way I could get the information I needed.

I decided that it would be nice to take a short vacation trip to West Virginia for the Columbus Day holiday and to stop at Emmitsburg, MD on our return home. I went in person to St. Joseph's rectory. At first they told me that they could not help me and seemed a little embarrassed about the whole matter. However, when I persisted, one of the priests suggested that I get in touch with the Mission of Mercy. He told me that Gianna was associated with it. This was the first time that I had heard about the Mission of Mercy and I did not know that Gianna was the founder. Of course, I was then able to write to Gianna and get her permission to put the Lessons on the World Wide Web.

In 2002, knowing that they were no longer holding prayer meetings in St. Joseph Church in Emmitsburg, MD and that the public apparitions had been stopped, I nonetheless felt a special call to go there once again. On July 29, 2002, having attended a family gathering in Lancaster, PA, my husband and I decided to make a side trip to the National Shrine Grotto of Our Lady of Lourdes in

Emmitsburg, MD before going home to New Jersey. Our Lady had said to Gianna that Emmitsburg was the Center of her Immaculate Heart, a refuge for all Mary's children all over the world. And I wanted to show my respect for her as Our Lady of Emmitsburg. We went early in the morning to the beautiful and serene Grotto of Our Lady of Lourdes where Saint Elizabeth Ann Seton and her companions spent their Sundays. While we were there, we visited the Chapel. As we left, I picked up a handout that contained the 'CHAPLIN'S MEDITATIONS…The EndTimes,' dated July 28, 2002.

In the Chapel handout, the writer refers to the fastest-selling adult fiction series ever, the *Left Behind* novels by Tim LaHaye and Jerry Jenkins. I had read an article about them in Newsweek Magazine. Apparently they have sold anywhere from 43,000,000 to 60,000,000 copies and a number of books in the series have made it to the Best Seller lists. Themes and symbols from the Book of Revelation are the foundation of this series, including the Second Coming, the Tribulation and the Antichrist. And in these books the 'Rapture' is a given. In the Chapel handout it is noted that: "the Catholic Church – and most Christians till the last century – never believed in anything called 'rapture.' And millenarianism – proposing a literal thousand year reign of Christ before a general judgment – has been condemned by the Church." In the Chaplin's 'meditations' on the Book of Revelation, he points out that: "what the saints, popes and doctors of the Church say (about the Book of Revelations) is still 'up for debate' [i.e., many symbolic elements in the Book]." He also stresses the major themes of the Book as seen from the Catholic perspective, including "repenting from sin and turning to our 'first love,' Jesus Christ – Rv.2: 4."

I basically agree with all of the things that the Chaplin wrote; and I believe that when the Chaplin states that "what the saints, popes and doctors of the Church say (about the

Book of Revelations) is still 'up for debate,'" this position gives catholics a certain latitude in interpretation. I find it very convincing when Mary, the Mother of God, says on June 29, 2000 that her message regarding the Second Coming of her son, the Child Jesus, to usher in His Kingdom, "has been foretold for many centuries and is not a new theology!" There are so many messages both in Vassula's writings and in Gianna's writings about this Second Coming, that it seems to me that it behooves all of us to give them serious consideration.

Moreover, I believe that when we pray the Our Father and say "thy kingdom come, thy will be done on earth as it is in heaven" (Matt. 6:10) we are praying for this Second Coming! I believe that this Second Coming, which is also called the Eucharistic Reign or the second Pentecost has been predicted in the Book of Revelations. And I believe that when this Eucharistic Reign occurs that the Protestant, Catholic and Orthodox churches will be united in a way that is not clear to me, but they will be united. The Immaculate Heart of Mary will triumph with her Son. Peace will come to the world and goodness will shine forth for all to see as God's will is "done on earth as it is in heaven." (Matt. 6:10)

This may seem farfetched to many. But for me it does not seem so at all! For I see it in a mystical way. In her book, *Way of Perfection*, St. Teresa of Avila discusses the prayer, the Our Father, as it relates to contemplation. When she comes to the words "Thy kingdom come" (Matt. 6:10) she describes the 'Prayer of Quiet' in these beautiful words: "They are so close to God that they know they can make themselves understood by signs. They are in the palace, near to their King, and they see that He is already beginning to give them *His Kingdom on earth.*"[20] (emphasis mine) I never was quite sure what these words of Jesus relating to the coming of the Kingdom meant. I remember reading St. Teresa of Avila and thinking that what she said was interesting. However, I soon forgot about them. They came back to me in full force when I became acquainted with the statements of the modern day visionaries about the Second Coming.

In the very next chapter, St. Teresa addresses the next words in the *paternoster*, "thy will be done on earth as it is in heaven." (Matt. 6:10) She says that this petition is fulfilled in the contemplative who has given her will entirely to the Lord. She says: "For since my earth has now become Heaven, it will be possible for Thy will to be done in me."[21] Teresa speaks of the importance of giving our will, which she refers to as a jewel, totally to God. She urges her sisters in religion: "Let us give Him once and for all the jewel which we have so often undertaken to give Him. For the truth is that He gives it to us first so that we may give it back to Him."[22]

Since, in these times through His prophets, God is calling everyone to mystical contemplation, I believe that by the power of the Holy Spirit, it will be these many blessed souls who will bring to fruition the words John heard from the throne:

> "Now at last God has his dwelling among men! He will dwell among them and they shall be his people, and God himself will be with them." And their dwelling place will be the "holy city of Jerusalem coming down out of heaven from God." And "I saw no temple in the city; for its temple was the sovereign Lord God and the Lamb. And the city had no need of sun or moon to shine upon it; for the glory of God gave it light, and its light is the Lamb." (Rev. 21:3, 10, 22-23)

If these words do, indeed, give some inkling as to what God really plans, the question arises, "Why?" The answer that I find most satisfying reminds me of the "Golden Age of Greece." Though this period of Ancient History lasted for a century or less, it laid the foundation for western civilization.

Due to the amazing achievements in art, philosophy, architecture, and literature, many classical scholars refer to this pinnacle in Greek history as the “Greek miracle.” In a similar manner, I can picture this dawning springtime of the Church, this Second Pentecost, as being seen by church historians as the “Golden Age of the Church” whose purpose it was to lay the foundation for the fulfilment of God’s Salvation Plan.

As I indicated earlier, there was no official web site associated with Our Lady of Emmitsburg until very recently, I therefore had difficulty getting information regarding Gianna. I bought each of the six *I am your JESUS of MERCY* books as soon as I was aware they were available. Later, I bought Dom Forker’s book, *Our Lady of Emmitsburg*. From time to time I searched the internet for news of Gianna, but found very little information. Then one day I suddenly came upon Our Lady of Emmitsburg’s new web site: http://www.CenteroftheImmaculateHeart.org. It is a very comprehensive web site as can been seen from their Site Map. I highly recommend it to anyone interested in learning more than the brief information I provide.

On the web site is an Introduction by Fr. Kieran Kavanaugh, O.C.D. to the **Words of God the Father for the World** given through Gianna Sullivan. Fr. Kieran is serving as spiritual advisor to Gianna relative to these messages from God the Father. Fr. Kieran translated the comprehensive writings of both St. Teresa of Avila and St. John of the Cross into English and is also involved in the Institute of Carmelite Studies.

In his Introduction, Fr. Kieran describes how, since December 2003, Our Lady has spoken frequently about God the Father. In particular, she has constantly pleaded that He would intervene in a personal way in our world. Fr. Kieran writes that: “On April 10, 2005, **Our Lady** said to Gianna: ‘It is now necessary to develop a Foundation here at the

Center of my Immaculate Heart.'" Fr. Kieran adds that on the Vigil of Trinity Sunday, May 21, 2005, Our Lady tells Gianna:

> "The title of this Foundation is the ***Foundation of the Sorrowful and Immaculate Heart of Mary.*** This Foundation belongs to **God the Father.** I, a beloved and most humble servant of God and the Spouse of the Holy Spirit, obeyed **God the Father;** and now, as an open vessel, just as you too are, I desire the world to know the ***Words of God the Father.***
>
> "The mission of this Foundation is to promulgate the Father's Words and the Truth of my Sorrowful and Immaculate Heart. In this Truth you shall see Our Two Hearts, my Son's and my own, formed into One, where the Crown of Thorns and the sword that pierced my Heart shall become the Crown of Glory."

The first message from God the Father was given in an auditory locution to Gianna on Trinity Sunday, May 22, 2005. This and subsequent monthly messages are published on the Foundation's web site. (CenteroftheImmaculateHeart.org). In the message from God the Father given to Gianna for publication on Feb. 8, 2007, God addresses the question discussed above, relative to the ***amount of time there now remains for humanity to respond to His call.*** It is now almost 20 years that Gianna has been receiving messages; and in this particular message the amount of time remaining is defined differently from previous messages. Note, especially, these words from God the Father: "there is not time to despair or to spare!"

> "Dear Children of Humanity,
>
> "I love you as your Father; and most importantly, I have given you everything that is good.
>
> "If you come to Me with open hearts, all is made anew. If you come, even with skepticism, I can make

all anew. But if you come blaspheming, **especially blaspheming the tremendous gift of the Holy Spirit**, then you cannot be made anew. You cannot desire evil, for you must desire love and that which is pure…

“You think that there is time to spare; but if you look within your lives and at what you yourself have done, there is not time to despair or to spare. There is only time to be made anew and to be cleansed…

“Those of you who desire to live your lives in your own way now, instead of as your soul was created to be, enjoy it; but do not ask why the Truth was not presented to you, for I have outlined the entire Truth. It is your free will that has rejected it.

“I remain faithful, at all costs.

The choice is yours.” (Emphasis mine)

SEVENTEEN

SECOND COMING

For a long time I had problems understanding and appreciating the role of the prophets in Scripture. In the Old Testament the first prophet who comes to my mind is Jonah, who was trying to escape from the Lord and ended up in the belly of a whale for three days! It is often said that the role of a prophet is a thankless one and Jonah is cited as an example. The reason for this, of course, is that when Jonah finally did as the Lord instructed and warned the people of Nineveh that their city would be destroyed in 40 days if they did not repent, the people of Nineveh did, in fact, repent; and the Lord relented and spared the city. The story of Jonah and of other prophets made me think that that was their major role, that is, to warn people that their wickedness would bring God's wrath down upon them if they didn't change.

Because Vassula Ryden and Gianna Sullivan are sometimes referred to as prophets, I wanted to find out more regarding the nature of prophecy. From the *Catechism of the Catholic Church*, I learned that it is the Catholic position that: "Through the prophets, God forms his people in the hope of salvation, in the expectation of a new and everlasting Covenant intended for all, to be written on their hearts." (Catechism #64) In other words, from a theological view, prophecy refers to the truths revealed by Christ himself which is God's revelation to us. This is further explained in the Catechism, in that when the Church speaks of prophets, it is referring, not just to the prophetic books, but to the writings of all of the authors of both the Old and New

Testament books. As I read this I realized that prophecy had a much broader meaning then I had realized.

Wishing to learn more, I read a fascinating speech titled, "Prophecy and Revelation," by the theologian Dr. Niels C. Hvidt, which was given in a conference in Cattolica, Sept. 18-21, 1998. This presentation can be found on the True Life in God web site. One particularly enlightening discussion in his speech concerned the question 'In what sense could it be said that Revelation ended with the last apostle?' He points out that one often hears the words of Martin Luther quoted to the effect that "We do not need any prophets, because God has spoken through his Son and therefore he has nothing more to say." It is my understanding that the teachings of the Catholic Church are similar.

Dr. Hvidt makes a very strong argument that prophets continued to play an important role in the New Testament and that until the end of the second century it was actually an "office in the Church;" that up until that time the "Church was guided both by priests and prophets." He further points out that concurrently, Church authority tended to be charismatic and was "based on the immediate experience of the Heavenly Christ through the prophets." Dr. Hvidt believes that because of the negative affects on the Church created by a number of false prophets who arose at that time, the Church moved away from its charismatic, vertical type of authority. In its place there developed a "more horizontal authority, based on the historical recollection of the life and teachings of the historical Jesus." This is the Church of today. The role of the prophet has been down played. Niels Hvidt notes that "Few theological topics have been covered so poorly as Christian prophecy. Such theologians as Karl Rahner, Hans Urs von Balthasar and Joseph Ratzinger (Pope Benedict XVI) have lamented this almost blank space on the theological chart."

There is another major point which Dr. Hvidt makes, which I found absolutely fascinating. He says that during the Second Vatican Council the idea of a *"personalistic approach to revelation"* was discussed. He believes that the previous position that revelation ended with the last apostle was discerned to be "an incomplete picture of revelation." This was based on the idea that "the word *end* was a faulty translation of the Latin *completare* which…does not mean to end but to fulfill – Christ is the fulfilled revelation of God ***but not its last manifestation."*** (bold italics mine) This idea presents a powerful new way to approach the totality of the implications inherent in this expanded definition! And, if pursued further, it seems to me that it could have a very beneficial impact on the Church.

Sometime in the middle to late 90's, Dr. Hvidt conducted an interview with Joseph Cardinal Ratzinger on 'The Problem of Christian Prophecy.' This interview is published on the True Life in God web site. In the introduction to the interview, Niels Hvidt repeats his position that Church theologians have spent little time in developing a theology of Christian prophecy. As a matter of fact, he even quotes, in the speech he gave in Cattolica, mentioned earlier in this chapter, the words of Rino Fisichella on prophecy in which he says that: "confronting the topic of Christian prophecy is like contemplating wreckage after a shipwreck."!!!

In the Introduction to his interview with Cardinal Ratzinger (Pope Benedict XVI), Dr. Hvidt goes on to discuss the relationship between Revelation and prophecy. He points out that Cardinal Ratzinger, in his capacity as a theologian, has spent considerable time addressing the concept of Revelation in great depth. According to Niels Hvidt, the Cardinal arrived at the following conclusion after studying the works of St. Bonaventura, that "the Revelation refers to the action of God in history in which the truth is gradually unveiled. The Revelation is the continuous growth of the Church in the fullness of the Logos." The Cardinal's idea that the Revelation is not fixed in time, but rather continues to grow as part and parcel of the history of the Church, gives me a new insight into the role of private revelations in relationship to today's prophets. In a very strong statement concerning the relationship between Revelation and prophecy, Dr. Hvidt makes it very clear that, in his opinion, "Any theological definition of Christian prophecy may only be arrived at within the context of this dynamic concept of Revelation."

How then are we to interpret the role of modern day prophets such as Gianna Sullivan and Vassula Ryden as seen in this light? In order to answer this it is necessary to have some understanding of what prophecy is and what its role in Christianity is. In the interview, Cardinal Ratzinger gives a very clear definition. He says: "The prophet is not a soothsayer. The essential element of the prophet is not the prediction of future events; the prophet is someone who tells the truth on the strength of his contact with God; the truth for today which also, naturally, sheds light on the future. It is not a question of foretelling the future in detail, but of rendering the truth of God present at this moment in time and of pointing us in the right direction."

Dr. Hvidt asks the Cardinal whether he thinks that future prophetic claims which occur after the death of the last apostle have any validity. The Cardinal gives a surprising answer. He actually says that the thesis that the Revelation ended with the last apostle "harbors a double misunderstanding. First of all, it harbors the idea that the prophet, who is essentially associated with the dimension of hope, has no further function…This is an error, because Christ came in the flesh and then rose again 'in the Holy Spirit.' This new presence of Christ in history, in the sacrament, in the Word, in the life of the Church, in the heart of every man is the expression and beginning of the definitive advent of Christ who 'fills all things.'(Eph. 4:11)…The concept that Christianity is already a totally complete presence and that it does not carry any structure of hope within it is the first error to be rejected."

The Cardinal then addresses the second misunderstanding, which he claims "is the reductive intellectual-type of conception of the Revelation, seen as a treasure of pieces of knowledge transmitted, to which nothing more can be added, totally complete." He continues with a beautiful explanation of our unfolding encounter with God. He refers to Jesus' 'Farewell Discourse' in John's Gospel which occurred during the Last Supper. He says that Christ explained that "his coming in the flesh was just a first step." Cardinal Ratzinger makes the point that the real coming happens

> "when he comes to all of us in the Spirit as the Risen One, so that entering into the truth may also acquire more and more profundity. It seems clear to me (the Cardinal) that considering that the time of the Church, that is, the time when Christ comes to us in Spirit is determined by this very pneumatological Christology – the prophetic element, as element of hope and appeal, cannot naturally be lacking or allowed to fade away."

Further on in the interview, Dr. Hvidt asks Cardinal Ratzinger whether it is a legitimate question as to whether the prophets "might have something radically new to say in the history of the Church and as regards theology itself?" The Cardinal gives an interesting answer, in that he points out how the prophetic figure of St. Dominic played a vital role in St. Thomas' development of his theological positions. He goes on to say: "The same could be said of Bonaventura and Francis of Assisi; the same holds for Hans Urs von Balthasar who is unthinkable without Adrienne von Speyr. I believe that it can be proven that for all the great theologians any new theological elaboration is only possible if the prophetic element has first paved the way."

As I consider these words of Joseph Cardinal Ratzinger, now Pope Benedict XVI, I cannot help but wonder what history will have to say about Gianna Sullivan and Vassula Ryden. Will history show us that these two mystics and prophets played a major role in advancing the development of the theology of the Holy Spirit and the theology of God the Father?

In his book, *Vassula of the Sacred Heart's Passion*, the noted theologian and author, Fr. Michael O'Carroll C.S.S.p., gave me a very enlightening insight into some of these topics. In his fourth chapter on 'The Holy Spirit' he points out that the Spirit has "been neglected in the Latin Church."[1] He supports this assertion by pointing out that prior to the start of Vatican II, on being asked to help set up an agenda, neither the bishops of the Church nor the Catholic universities mentioned the Holy Spirit in their response. Then, before the start of the fourth session, a Greek theologian, Nikos Nissiotis, wrote an article for The Ecumenical Review in which he commented that: "the texts issued or being considered would have little impact in the Orthodox churches, as they said nothing significant about the Holy Spirit."[2] Whether or not this comment was effective, the fact remains that the fourth session did address the subject of the Holy Spirit.

An interesting point that Fr. O'Carroll makes is that Pope John Paul II published more on the theology of the Holy Spirit than any of his predecessors. He indicates that there are two ideas, in particular, which are increasingly coming to the fore in theological thinking: "the role of the Spirit in the life of Jesus, and his central influence in the Church's missionary activity."[3] Fr. O'Carroll quotes a very profound statement that John Paul II made relative to the Spirit's activity in the life of Christ. The Pope's statement gave me a new insight into the role that the theologians play in elaborating on the life of Christ. John Paul II writes:

> "the time has come to emphasize the fact that the first and greatest wonder accomplished by the Holy Spirit is Christ Himself...This means that not only is the Holy Spirit's light necessary for penetrating Christ's mystery, but the influence of the Holy Spirit in the Incarnation of the Word and in the entire life of Christ must be taken into account to explain the Jesus of the Gospel. The Holy Spirit left the mark of His own personality on the face of Christ."[4]

Father O'Carroll feels that John Paul II's teachings on the Holy Spirit have not reached the faithful. He quotes many of the beautiful messages in *True Life in God*(TLIG) which relate to the Holy Spirit and to John Paul's teachings. He says that these teachings of John Paul: "must be brought into the lives of the faithful, becoming dynamic, motivating conduct. Those called to such a task will find the writings of Vassula helpful, illuminating in theory and practice."[5] Personally, these messages of TLIG have a tremendous impact on me! Here is just one quote on the role of the Holy Spirit:

> "Look, look around you, My Holy Spirit comes to meet you and revive you all. Dressed as a beggar, with tears of blood streaming down My cheeks, I descend from My throne, leaning all the way to you, to save your soul from disaster and from famine. For the sake of My Name I shall demonstrate Myself through these very things you do not believe any more. I shall demonstrate My Holy Spirit through marvels, through miracles. I shall demonstrate My power through weakness and wretchedness as never before. I shall come with thousands of myriads of angels to pour on you, generation, My celestial Manna, this hidden Manna [Rev. 2:17] and fill your mouth with My food so that your mouth proclaims My Glory."[6]

Additionally, in his book, Father O'Carroll indicates that present day theologians are beginning to be aware that "there is a need to develop a theology of God the Father."[7] One of the major reasons he cites for this is the fact that in this present age the divinity of Jesus Christ is being called into question. He goes on to discuss the relationship between the Father and Son and points out that "Jesus effected a total innovation in doctrine and prayer centered on the Father, His *Abba.*"[8] He then discusses the messages given to Vassula Ryden by Jesus. He makes the amazing claim that: "In the messages given by Him (Jesus) to Vassula we reach a summit when we study the revelation He makes of the Father, when we meet the words spoken to her by the Father."[9] Here is one example of the words of God the Father to Vassula:

> "Tell them that I am the most tender Father; tell them how I lean to reach them now. Love and loyalty now descend to embrace all of you, to renew you, to revive you and lift you up from the lethargy that covers this earth; do not say that I am too far to reach, unmoved by your misery and unresponsive to your calls; if the flames lick up your countries and fires devour the people of the earth it is all due to the great apostasy that seized nation after nation infiltrating in the heart of My law; this apostasy beggared you and made you believe you are fatherless…how I pity you! My warnings and My calls echo the earth and though My grief is acute and My justice now brimming over, I can still relent and I can accept the homage you would offer Me; I am ready to forgive you through the blood shed by My Son and through His sacrifice, if you take My words to heart. I who created you out of love ask you: will I hear from you your cry of repentance?"[10]

This emphasis on God the Father is also most pronounced in the recent messages that Dr. Gianna Sullivan is receiving. In particular the messages she has reported from

God the Father. At first I had difficulty in understanding the import of this new happening in Emmitsburg, MD. I was glad that there finally was a web site which would make known to the whole world the existence of these messages from God and from Our Lady. But I wondered about the words of Our Lady to Gianna on May 21, 2005, which I quoted in the previous chapter. Our Lady tells her to start a Foundation to be called the Foundation of the Sorrowful and Immaculate Heart of Mary, and further, that "This Foundation belongs to God the Father."

My first thought was that God the Father was really serious and was going to give us the 'what for.' But now, in retrospect, it seems to me that this Foundation and the words from God the Father, are intended to be one more, and perhaps in our era, the final way which God is using to give us a fatherly warning of what is to come. And to once again tell us that He is a God of Love! And to tell us about our mother, Mary, the Mother of God.

In the first message of God the Father given on May 22, 2005, Trinity Sunday, for release on Dec. 8, 2005, The Feast of the Immaculate Conception of Mary, God the Father reveals how "the Triune God, Father, Son and Holy Spirit, the Holy Trinity, gathered together. In this meeting Creation unfolded; and the Eyes of this Triune Godhead, the Father, released a plan of Goodness and Joy, filled with all the good works that were to unfold in this Creation." However, knowing that man would rebel against God, the Father says: "From the inception of this most beautiful Plan of the Holy Trinity, it was determined that My Son would later come in human flesh to redeem the world which, created by My Hands, would come back to Me."

I wondered why the name of the Foundation was called 'Foundation of the Sorrowful and Immaculate Heart of Mary.' God the Father explains why. "There at the same time was created the most beautiful, sinless Immaculate

Soul, whose Heart would be pierced with a sword. This sword would not only pierce her Heart, but also the hearts of those who would follow her. She was always the Sorrowful and Immaculate Heart who had dedicated her life to the Truth. No women has ever been created, nor shall ever be created, as pure and holy as this most Immaculate Virgin."

Later in this message God the Father tells us how much He loves us. He says: "I am a loving God, a holy God. I am your God. There is only One. There shall never be another. The Mercy I give to you is the Mercy from the Womb, the Womb where my Son first became Flesh. I am a God of kindness, and I am a God Who is loyal and faithful to those who love the Truth."

As I read the writings of these two mystics, Gianna Sullivan and Vassula Ryden, I slowly came to the conviction that God has a plan for our era and that the Bible contains information pertaining to that plan. I used to think that God's Salvation Plan for us was already complete; that it consisted of the life, death and resurrection of Jesus Christ. But just as I now believe that the meaning of Revelation is continuing to unfold and to be made clearer to us through the present day prophets, I also think that God's Salvific Plan is still unfolding. And I believe that it is spelled out in the Book of Revelation as well as certain other books of the Bible.

What I am referring to is my belief that Jesus will come again to this earth, to the New Jerusalem, but not in His physical body. Instead, He will manifest Himself in a Spiritual Eucharistic Reign to the whole world. Most of what I have read and thought about relative to the Second Coming is based on the messages that both Gianna Sullivan and Vassula Ryden received. While what they said was more than impressive, initially I found it most puzzling and did not know what to make of their teachings. For example, here is an excerpt from a message that Our Lady gave to Gianna on March 2, 2000:

> "It is the unveiling of God's Mercy which will lift this world out of its misery. Jesus will come a second time and reign. He is coming and it will be the return of Jesus as a Child to enlighten the minds and hearts of all people, of all faiths, of all nations, and of every race...His Kingdom shall be an era of peace...My Son will unveil His Mercy to the world, but He will ***not*** walk on the world as you know it...It will ***not*** be His Final Judgment and Coming, for this next era will be the Covenant of Our Two Hearts, a spiritual Eucharistic Reign where the Child Jesus will usher in a Kingdom of Peace."

Another example is the message that Vassula received from Our Lady relative to the Second Pentecost. Mary says: "today, I invite you all to pray with fervor for the renewal of the Church, for the second Coming of the Lord: for the second Pentecost; this is why Jesus and I come today in various countries to prepare you all for this Coming; pray and lead a life of adoration, pray for the conversion of souls so that everyone may be ready for the Lords's Return; Love is on the Way of Return, listen and you will already hear His Footsteps;" (TLIG 4-22-1990)

This was very heavy stuff. What was I to make of such claims? Since I didn't understand, I just let it be. I reasoned that what was being said was symbolic. If God wanted me to understand, He would help me understand. To me, the main thing was always the fact that God was speaking to us through these visionaries; that He loved us more than I had ever imagined; and that He was calling everyone to mystical contemplation. Much later, I came upon two articles by Fr. James Fannan, PIME. He is the priest who was Vassula's first spiritual counselor in Bangladesh. He is the one whose initial reaction to Vassula, when she sought help and guidance, was to tell her that it was the work of Satan!

It is interesting to note how Vassula responded to this severe criticism. In the book, *The Vassula Enigma*, she tells the author, Jacques Neirynck, how she reacted to the words of Fr. Fannan. She tells him that, since not only she, but also her friends had been converted, she felt that only God could do that. She answers simply that "I was very disappointed with the first contact with Father James. I went home. Then I said to God: 'If it is really You, God the Father, whom I am meeting, may this priest, this one at least, not all the others, may this priest tell me one day that my messages are from God. And then I will no longer have doubts, I will know that you are God.'" In response the Father says these strong and reassuring words: "I will make him bend."[11]

In an article which I found on the TLIG web site, written by Fr. Fannan, titled A Light shed on the Three and a Half Years of rebellion and the Two Witnesses (Rv. 11:2), he makes a number of interesting points. He says that it is clear from the TLIG Messages that the "two witnesses are symbolic names for the Sacred Hearts of Jesus and Mary." He quotes these words from the message of Dec. 24, 1991: "Elijah and Moses have come already and you have not recognized them but treated them as you pleased. You have not listened to Our Two Hearts, the Immaculate Heart of My Mother and My Sacred Heart…"

Another interesting point that he makes is that the "three and a half year period of iniquity has come to an end" and that, according to Vassula, "many of the prophecies made in *True Life in God* have already been accomplished, but no one noticed!" He says that we need to see things as God sees them. He claims that "The Apocalypse is full of catastrophic events, but many of these are taking place on a spiritual level and we are therefore unaware of them."

To explain the many catastrophic words in the Apocalypse, he uses the message of Sept.15, 1991 relative to the 'Purification' which has been foretold, not just by

Vassula, but also by Gianna Sullivan and the visionaries of Garabandal. He compresses the key points of this message regarding the experience of each soul during the Purification as follows: "I will allow your soul to perceive all the events of your lifetime…you will realize how much innocent blood your sins shed from victim souls…shriveled with your awakening, your eyes will be transfixed in Mine…you will tremble and shudder when you see yourself as a decaying corpse, devastated by worm and vulture…pray for the sinner who is unaware of his decay." Fr. Fannan sums up Vassula's role in the history of salvation in these amazing words:

> "She (Vassula) has a ministry to restore Christian unity and ultimately the kingdom of God on earth. Moreover, like the prophets of old, her ministry, *True Life in God,* will continue to nourish souls till the end of the world. It is truly a classic for all times, and a guidebook to living in the new era of peace of Fatima, which is certainly the era of peace of the Apocalypse, the 'thousand years' of Millennium."

Fr. Fannan writes of this 'thousand year' period in a three-part article which is available on the TLIG web site in the Newsletter section under the following dates: Jan. 19, 21, 23, 1999. The article is titled Millenarianism and Prophecy. He tells us that the article resulted from "many personal conversations and almost eight years of study of the writings of a now well-known personality in the world of ecumenism, Vassula Ryden." He says that, although he originally rejected Vassula's messages, his acceptance of her writings was based on the fact that they were in accord with the teachings of the Church as he understood them at that time. He describes how, as time went on, he kept finding in her writings fresh insights. He began to realize that these 'fresh insights' were actually "reminders of things that are found in the early writings of the Church" that were "classical teachings of the Fathers of the Church or the Scriptures themselves…"

What did Fr. Fannan learn from this study? Or rather, what did I learn from this article which is so well documented, and contains so many quotes from, and explanations based on at least ten different books of the New Testament as well as two books in the Old Testament? In addition to Scripture, Fr. Fannan investigated what the early Church Fathers had to say about this subject.

It is fascinating to read St. Justin's belief in the Second Coming, or as he refers to it, the new Jerusalem. This new Jerusalem is referred to in Scripture in the following extraordinarily symbolic terms: "Then I saw a new heaven and a new earth, for the first heaven and the first earth had vanished, and there was no longer any sea. I saw the holy city, new Jerusalem, coming down out of heaven from God, made ready like a bride adorned for her husband." (Rev. 21:1-2) Fr. Fannan quotes from St. Justin's famous work, *Dialogue with Trypho, the Jew*. Trypho asks St. Justin if he believes that Jerusalem will be rebuilt. St. Justin responds that he is 'absolutely' convinced that it will be, although "there are many Christians of pure and pious faith who do not share this belief. But I and such other Christians as judge rightly everything, believe that there will be…a thousand years in which Jerusalem will be built up, adorned and enlarged, as the prophets Ezechiel and Isaiah and others declare.[Chapter 80]"

Fr. Fannan points out that "the idea that Jesus and the ancient Church saw the Messianic era or 'parousia' as imminent is not a new one." However, this belief gradually died away, and as Fr. Fannan says: "For some modern Catholics the idea that there could be any sort of interim period of peace or 'triumph of good over evil' seems utterly fantastic" I certainly belonged in this category. I have frequently found that any profound idea that is new to me or any concept that I have never heard before, often seems incomprehensible the first time I hear about it. However, the second time around, it usually becomes understandable; but, if it is very complex it may require much more time. This has certainly been the case in my understanding and belief in, what is often called the Second Coming, the Parousia or the Eucharistic Reign! It was not until I read this article by Fr. Fannan that I began to feel that I had some understanding of what the prophets of our era are talking about!

Now, as I look back over the years since my early retirement in 1988, I am amazed at how I have grown spiritually. In particular, how my understanding of spiritual matters has developed. God acts in many different ways. In my case He has used contemporary prophets to enlighten me. What attracted me most in these inspired messages was the emphasis placed on mystical contemplation. But what I have learned goes far beyond anything I could have conceived of! The unifying concept that stands out in my mind is the rabbinical teaching that Sister H. addressed in her article, Recognizably Jewish, which I covered in Chapter 14. Sister H. wrote of the absence of grammar in Biblical Hebrew as well as the use of the word 'and' at the beginning of each verse. She points out that this lack of grammar is seen as manifesting "that the work of God from the beginning of creation and all salvation history is one continuous unfolding act of God and is therefore expressed by one continuous sentence." This concept made a tremendous impression on me! I began to appreciate how God's plan is ongoing. Many of the things that puzzled me in both the Old and New Testaments, as well as in the inspired writings of the modern day mystics and visionaries, slowly appeared in a new light.

As I read the message from God the Father to Gianna Sullivan, dated May 22, 2005, in which He describes how the Triune God, Father, Son and Holy Spirit gathered together and "released a plan of Goodness and Joy," I understood, in a way I never had before, how God's Salvation Plan began on day one. And I began to appreciate how this God of Abraham, of Isaac and Jacob had His own mysterious reasons for slowly revealing Himself to mankind.

And the Biblical passage "In the beginning, was the Word, and the Word was with God, and the Word was God." (John 1:1-2) and the "Word became flesh," (John 1:14), which always meant so much to me, took on a more profound meaning. And I became convinced that Jesus' words, which seemed ever to hover in my subconscious: "I have come to set fire to the earth, and how I wish it were already kindled." (Luke 12:49), that these words did relate to the Book of Revelation. And now I believe as Vassula says, that the ***End of Times*** does not mean the end of the world! Rather, it refers to the end of an era or epoch. And I look forward with joy to the spiritual Second Coming of Jesus and the new springtime of Christ's Church.

When I retired, the one thing that I never expected, was that my spiritual journey would involve an in depth study of both private revelations and mystical phenomena! Never, in a million years, would I have ever guessed that these two topics were matters that would occupy a considerable amount of my time and effort. As I have said repeatedly, my interest was in mystical contemplation, not mystical phenomena such as visions and locutions. However, I was concerned as to whether or not mystical phenomena was a necessary part of mystical contemplation. Further, I was concerned that the teaching of the Catholic Church over the last several hundred years, as Father Keating has said, emphasized that contemplation was only for a few select souls and was not to be sought after by the typical priest or religious. And certainly, it was not for the laity! In retrospect, all I can think of is to thank God. Not only did He provide answers to my questions in a most unusual and encouraging way, but He provided me with consoling insights into His most extraordinary Salvation Plan. A plan that is ongoing throughout history and involves God's intimate involvement in our lives.

Here and there in this book, I have indicated that there were a number of issues that I was puzzled about; and that were not resolved for me at the specific period of time of which I was writing. In Chapter Six on the apparitions in Scottsdale, AZ, I mentioned a message from Jesus in which He urges the members of the Thursday Night Prayer group to say 'Yes' once again since it was so important to His plan. Jesus almost pleads with them as He says: "Please, believe when I say to you, your 'yes' is crucial to My plan, which is My mother's plan."[12] As I indicated above, I now believe that Jesus's plan is part of His ongoing Salvation Plan and relates to the Second Coming.

Is there a difference between Mary's plan and her Son's plan? Jesus says they are the same. But that seems to negate anything personal about Mary's plan. I tend to think that God respects each person's unique individuality and in that sense Mary has concentrated on doing certain things to help her Son fulfill His plan. And I think that probably what Jesus means is that Mary is 'one' with Him and that Mary's sole focus is on doing God's will. Regarding Mary's plan, I remember reading somewhere that Our Lady has indicated that she will appear in everyone's home, if that is necessary to bring us back to her Son!

Another outstanding issue is: What is happening in Scottsdale now? And: What has become of the eight young adults that Gianna saw in her dream? A partial answer is contained in the book, *My Dear Ones...MERCY.* It contains published messages which were given to the Friday Night Prayer group (not to be confused with the Thursday Night Prayer group) of St. Maria Goretti Roman Catholic Church, which is situated in the affluent area of Scottsdale in Phoenix, AZ. In the INTRODUCTION of the book, it reads that, as of 1994 the messages are given less frequently, and that the "prayer group has been called to live by faith."[13] I have just recently heard that the parish of St. Maria Goretti Church has become an exemplar of a Christian community!

Relative to Scottsdale, there is an important fact that is brought out in the book, *Our Lady of Emmitsburg*. Dom Forker points out that a very powerful message was given to Gianna in 1996. He says that in it Our Lady "symbolically summarized the mystical and miraculous role of the Cross of Jesus, His most compassionate symbol of mercy: 'His "Center of Divine Mercy" (Scottsdale) and this "Center of My Immaculate Heart" (Emmitsburg) will join the East and West in union with the covenant of the two hearts (the Sacred Heart of Jesus and the Immaculate Heart of Mary).' It is the horizontal beam of the Cross…Through the Cross, Evil's reign shall end."[14]

In the last Lesson of volume one of the *I am your JESUS of MERCY* books, Jesus points out that this is the 'Age of Divine Mercy.' Considering the emphasis on Scottsdale as the Center of Divine Mercy, I tend to think that there are many more spiritual happenings to come in Scottsdale.

In Chapter Five, where I discuss Mary's apparitions in Medjugorje and the devastating wars in Yugoslavia, I raised the question as to why Our Lady selected Medjugorje for her apparitions. When I read Mary Craig's book, *Sparks from Heaven*, I was fascinated how she explained that Bosnia-Hercegovina was in an area of the world where many civilizations, cultures and faiths had interacted, often violently, down through the centuries. She says that "It marked the historic divide between East and West."[15] I kept wondering about the East-West part. When I learned from Vassula Ryden's works, that God planned to unite the Orthodox Church and the Roman Catholic Church, the houses of the East and West, respectively, I couldn't help wonder if, perhaps, that was a symbolic part of Mary's plan. And, as Jesus says to Gianna, Mary's plan is part of God's plan. Do Mary's apparitions in Medjugorje, which continue to this day, somehow relate to the predicted unity between these two great Christian houses? I'm not sure, but it certainly seems likely to me.

In Chapter Eight I indicated that one of my concerns was whether mystical phenomena were a necessary part of contemplative prayer. As I grew up, I was a child of my time. I thought that anyone who had visions of Jesus or of Our Blessed Mother must be a very saintly person. Since I wasn't a saintly person and since I wanted nothing to do with visions, etc., why did I spend years reading all the writings of St. Teresa of Avila and St. John of the Cross? The only explanation that I can give is that I felt this continuous longing for God and these books spoke of God's accessability and soothed that longing. But I always felt a little uncomfortable about the visions, locutions, raptures, etc. which were described in their books.

Reading Fr. Thomas Keating's position that mystical phenomena are not an integral part of mystical contemplation put my mind at ease. My other question was whether, as St. Teresa seems to imply, a vision is a necessary part of the Spiritual Marriage? I now believe that St. Teresa's description of the spiritual marriage in her chapter on the Seventh Mansion should be taken as a description of her own experiences. I do not think that they should be viewed as the last word on mystical contemplation, even though she now has the title Doctor of the Church. It seems to me that God gave her these visions so that mystical theologians would get a fuller understanding of what transpires theologically in the spiritual marriage. But I do not think that such visions are necessary to everyone on this contemplative journey to God. I think it depends very much on the mission each person is given in this life and the trials and hardships they encounter as well as their personal needs.

The final question that I raised was: Is the call to contemplation universal? I have come to believe that the call to contemplation is universal; that God in His goodness has made mystical contemplation available, always, to everyone. Certainly, Father Thomas Keating seems to think so. Based on his writings and those of both Gianna Sullivan and

Vassula Ryden, as well as my own inner convictions, I believe that God, particularly in this period of history, in His inscrutable wisdom is calling everyone in the entire world to be united with the Triune Godhead while we are still in this earthly life.

How could I doubt this when, in so many countless messages, Jesus keeps telling us how much He loves us and how much He wants us to love Him? It is my understanding that, if we do not reach the transforming union in this life, all who die in God's grace will become one with God, as soon as the soul's purification is completed in purgatory. That is the divine beatitude to which He calls us! And to which He invites us to participate in while we are still here on earth!

Today, as never before, God calls us to this transforming union in the many messages He gives to our contemporary visionaries. One of the most touching and revealing passages that I have ever read is contained in a message to Vassula. As Jesus is speaking to Vassula, He slowly turns to look with a penetrating glance at each reader of His message. Then, addressing the reader directly, He tells the reader that he has not fully understood this Heavenly Treasure,

> "what is beyond all price…the tremendous grace of knowing Me in an intimate union and tasting interiorly, in the nuptial chamber of My Heart, My sweetness and my Divine kisses." Jesus continues, explaining that while good works, devotional prayers, acts of love, etc., are all good, He would **"be greatly disappointed that you would die before having known Me, I would be greatly distressed were you to die now before having understood Me;"** (TLIG 11-2-97) (emphasis mine)

BIBLIOGRAPHY

Chapter 2. THE UNEXPECTED

1. *Medjugorje,* published by the Riehle Foundation, Milford, Ohio, 1988, p.33.
2. Ibid., p.17.
3. Ibid.

Chapter 3. THE DARK NIGHT

1. *Open Mind, Open Heart* by Father Thomas Keating, published in Great Britain by Element Books Ltd., New Edition, 1992, p. 25.
2. *Medjugorje*, above cited, p. 54.
3. *Messages and Teachings of Mary at Medjugorje* by Father Rene Laurentin and Father Rene Lejeune, published by the Riehle Foundation, Milford, Ohio, 1988, p. 302.
4. Ibid., p. 304.
5. *Spark from Heaven* by Mary Craig, published by the Ave Maria Press, Notre Dame, Indiana, 1988, p. 58.
6. *Messages and Teachings of Mary at Medjugorje*, above cited, p. 173.

Chapter 4. MEDJUGORJE

1. *Spark from Heaven*, above cited, p. 19.
2. *Messages and Teachings of Mary at Medjugorje*, above cited, p. 150.

3. *Spark from Heaven*, above cited, p. 19

4. Ibid., p. 20.

Chapter 5. THE MYSTERY OF EVIL

1 *Newsweek*, December 17, 2001, "The Question That We Should Be Asking" by Alison Hornstein, p.14.

2. *Phi Kappa Phi FORUM*, Spring 2002, "Demonizing the United States" by Paul Trout, p .3.

3. *Newsweek*, August 19, 2002, "The Nature of Human Nature" by George F. Will, p. 64.

4. *Spark from Heaven*, above cited, p. 21.

5. Ibid., p. 29.

6. *The Balkans* by Misha Glenny, published by Viking Penguin, 2000, p. 500.

7. Ibid., p .623.

8. Ibid., p. XXIV.

9. *Charleston Gazette*, SC, May 8, 1999, "Balkan trap, Kosovo hate incurable", editorial by James A. Haught.

10. *Origins of a Catastrophe* by Warren Zimmermann, published by Random House, Inc., NY 1996, p. VII.

11. *The Balkans*, above cited, p. 661.

12. *I am your JESUS of MERCY*, Volume VI, Messages received by Dr. Gianna Talone-Sullivan, published by Queenship Publishing Company, Goleta, CA, 1999, p. 84.

Chapter 6. APPARITIONS IN SCOTTSDALE, AZ

1. *I am your JESUS of MERCY*, published by the Riehle Foundation, PO Box 7, Milford, Ohio 45150, 1989. Vol. 1, p. 9.

2. Ibid., p. 24.
3. Ibid., p. 109.
4. Ibid., p. 109.
5. Ibid., p. 111.
6. *Our Lord and Our Lady in Scottsdale* by Father Rene Laurentin, published by Faith Publishing CO., PO Box 237, Milford, Ohio 45150, 1992, p.14.
7. *Our Lord and Our Lady in Scottsdale*, above cited, p. 20.
8. Ibid., p. 21
9. *Our Lady of Emmitsburg* by Dom Forker, published by the Queenship Publishing CO., PO Box 220, Goleta, CA 93116, 2000, p. 19.
10. Ibid., p. 18.
11. Ibid., p. 35.
12. Ibid., p. 125.
13. *Our Lady Comes to Scottsdale, Is it Authentic?* by Robert Faricy, S.J. and Lucy Rooney, S.N.D. de N., published by the Riehle Foundation, PO Box 7, Milford, Ohio 45150, 1991, p. 6.
14. *Our Lady of Emmitsburg*, above cited, p. 20.
15. *Our Lord and Our Lady in Scottsdale*, above cited, p. 47.
16. *Our Lady of Emmitsburg*, above cited, p. 23.
17. *Our Lady Comes to Scottsdale, Is it Authentic*?, above cited, p. 13.
18. *Our Lady of Emmitsburg*, above cited, p. 3.
19. Ibid., p. 5.
20. Ibid., p. 6.

21. Ibid., p. 35.

22. Ibid., p. 39.

23. *I am your JESUS of MERCY*, Vol. 4, p. 108.

24. *Our Lady of Emmitsburg*, above cited, p. 60.

25. Ibid., p. 62.

26. *I am your JESUS of MERCY*, Vol. I, p. 134.

27. *Our Lord and Our Lady in Scottsdale*, above cited, p.35.

28. *Our Lady Comes to Scottsdale, Is it Authentic?*, p. 43.

29. *Our Lord and Our Lady in Scottsdale*, above cited, p. 28.

30. Ibid., p. 41.

31. Ibid., p. 39.

Chapter 7. SPIRITUAL MARRIAGE

1. *Reading the Old Testament* by Lawrence Boadt, published by the Paulist Press, NY, NY. 1984. p.485-6.

2. *The Mystics of the Church* by Evelyn Underhill, published by Schocken Books, NY, NY. 1964. p.86.

3. *Enduring Grace* by Carol Lee Flinders, published by Harper Collins Publishers, NY, NY. 1993. p. 2.

4. *Collected Works of St. John of the Cross*, translated by Kieran Kavanaugh, O.C.D. and Otilio Rodriguez, O.C.D., published by the Institute of Carmelite Studies, Washington, DC. 1979. p. 415.

5. *The Complete Works of St. John of the Cross*, translated and edited by E. Allison Peers, published by the Newman Press, Westminster, Maryland, 1953. Volume 2, p.134.

6. *Collected Works of St. John of the Cross,* above cited, p. 517.

7. *The Complete Works of St. Teresa of Jesus*, translated and edited by E. Allison Peers, published by Sheed & Ward, London and New York, 1946. Volume 2, p. 354.

8. Ibid., p.355.

9. Ibid., p.360.

10. Ibid.

11. *Catechism of the Catholic Church*, published by the Catholic Book Publishing CO., NY, NY. 1994. No. 1000.

12. *The Complete Works of St. John of the Cross*, above cited, Volume 2, p. 133.

13. Ibid., p 133.

14. Ibid., Volume 3, p. 29.

Chapter 8. MYSTICAL PHENOMENA

1. *The Complete Works of St. Teresa of Jesus*, above cited, Volume 2, p. 188.

2. Ibid., p. 279.

3. Ibid., p. 280.

4. Ibid., p. 287.

5. Ibid., p. 283.

6. Ibid., p. 310.

7. Ibid., p. 314.

8. Ibid., p. 316.

9. Ibid., p. 315.

10. Ibid., p. 346.

11. Ibid., p. 331.

12. Ibid., p. 334.

13. *The Complete of St. John of the Cross*, above cited, volume 1, p. 76.

14. *Collected Works of St. John of the Cross*, above cited, p. 156.

15. Ibid., p. 158.

16. *The Cloud of Unknowing*, newly edited, with an introduction by William Johnston, published by Doubleday, NY, NY. 1973. p. 140.

17. Ibid., p. 50.

18. Ibid., p. 71.

19. Ibid., p. 7.

20. Ibid., p. 8.

21. Ibid., p. 26.

Chapter 9. REVEALED TRUTHS

1. *Catechism of the Catholic Church*, above cited, No. 50.

2. Ibid., No. 121.

3. *Reading the Old Testament*, above cited, p. 167.

4. Ibid., p. 168.

Chapter 10. RATIONALISM

1. *Pocket Catholic Dictionary* by John A. Hardon, S.J., published by Doubleday, NY, NY., p. 359.

2. *Catholic Encyclopedia*, 1911, found on internet, Vol XII.

3. *True Life in God* by Vassula Ryden, printed edition, published by J.M.J. Publications, Belfast, Northern Ireland, 1991. p. 311.

4. *The God Delusion* by Richard Dawkins published by Houghton Mifflin Company, Boston and New York, 2006. p. 58.

5. Ibid., p. 67.

6. Ibid., p. 121.

7. Ibid., p. 315.

8. Ibid., p. 339.

Chapter 11. PHYSICISTS AND MYSTICS

1. *Mathematics and the Search for Knowledge* by Morris Kline, published by Oxford University Press, New York and Oxford, 1985. p. vi.

2. Ibid., p. 50.

3. Ibid., p. 85.

4. Ibid., p. 106.

5. Ibid., p. 122.

6. Ibid., p. 123.

7. Ibid., p. 146.

8. Ibid., p. 233.

9. *Quantum Questions* edited by Ken Wilber, published by Shambhala, Boston, 2001. p. ix.

10. Ibid.

11. Ibid.

12. Ibid., p. 56.

13. Ibid., p. 62.

14. *Mathematics and the Search for Knowledge*, above cited., p. 121.

15. Ibid., p. 121.

16. Ibid., p. 116.

17. *Quantum Questions*, above cited, p. 10.

18. Ibid., p. 14.

19. Ibid., p. 19.

20. Ibid., p. 11.

21. Ibid., p. 11.

22. *Mathematics and the Search for Knowledge*, above cited, p. 146.

23. *Relativity*, A Popular Exposition by Albert Einstein, published by Crown Publishers, Inc., New York, 1961, p. 57.

24. Ibid., p. 49.

25. *Quantum Questions*, above cited, p. 7.

26. Ibid., p. 8.

27. Ibid., p. 9.

Chapter 12. THE INVISIBLE WALL

1. *Intimacy with God* by Father Thomas Keating, published by Crossroad, 370 Lexington Avenue, NY, NY 10017, 1994, p. 68 .

2. *Open Mind, Open Heart* by Father Thomas Keating, published by Element Inc., 42 Broadway, Rockport, MA 01966, 1992, p. 20.

3. Ibid., p. 21.

4. Ibid.

5. Ibid.
6. Ibid., p. 24.
7. Ibid.
8. *Intimacy with God*, above cited, p. 14.
9. Ibid.
10. *Open Mind, Open Heart*, above cited, p. 27.
11. Ibid.
12. Ibid., p. 26.
13. Intimacy with God, above cited, p. 122.
14. Ibid., p. 125.
15. Ibid.
16. *Invitation to Love* by Father Thomas Keating, published by Element Inc., above cited, 1992, p. 14.
17. *Intimacy with God*, above cited, p. 16.
18. Ibid., p. 13.
19. Ibid., p. 15.
20. Ibid., p. 17.
21. Ibid., p. 18.

Chapter 13. MYSTICAL CONTEMPLATION

1. *Open Mind, Open Heart*, above cited, p. 13.
2. Ibid., p. 13.
3. Ibid., p. 15.
4. *Invitation to Love*, above cited, p. 103.
5. *Fruits and Gifts of the Spirit* by Father Thomas Keating, published by Lantern Books, One Union Sq. W., Suite 201, NY, NY 10003, 2000, p. 115.

6. Ibid., p. 115.

7. *Intimacy with God*, above cited, p. 115.

8. Ibid.

9. Ibid., above cited, p. 6.

10. Ibid., p. 8.

11. Ibid., p. 9.

12. Ibid.

13. *The Complete Works of St. John of the Cross*, above cited, vol. 1, p. 71.

14. Ibid., p. 87.

15. Ibid., p. 127.

16. Ibid., p. 182.

17. *Open Mind, Open Heart*, above cited, p. 9.

18. Ibid.

19. *The Complete Works of St. John of the Cross*, above cited, p. 13.

20. Ibid., p. 204.

21. *Varieties of Mystic Experience* by Elmer O'Brien, S.J., published by Holt, Rinehart and Winston, 1964, p. 12.

22. *Intimacy with God*, above cited, p. 126.

23. Ibid., p. 128.

24. Ibid., p. 129.

25. Ibid., p. 136.

Chapter 14. "RECOGNIZABLY JEWISH"

1. *The Two Witnesses* by Father Michael O'Carroll, C.S.Sp., published by the 101 Foundation Inc., PO

Box 151, Asbury, NJ 088802, 1996, p. 268.

2. True Life in God, vol. 12, Original Handwritten Edition, published by Trinitas, PO Box 475, Independence, Missouri 64051, 2003, p. 143.

3. Ibid., p. 317.

4. *My Angel Daniel*, Original Handwriting Edition by Vassula Ryden, published by Trinitas, above cited, Second Printing 2001, p. XIII.

5. *True Life in God*, vol. 12, above cited, p. III.

6. Ibid.

7. *The Vassula Enigma* by Jacques Neirynck, published by the English Assoc. of TLIG, PO Box 93, Wantage DO, OX12 8DQ, 2001, p. 20.

8. Ibid., p. 21.

9. *True Life in God*, vol. 12, above cited, P. XXXVIII.

10. *The Vassula Enigma*, above cited, p. 7.

11. Ibid.

12. Ibid., p. 13.

13. Ibid., p. 14.

Chapter 15. GOD'S LOVE HYMN

1. *The Vassula Enigma*, above cited, p. 14.

2. Ibid., p. 15.

3. Ibid.

4. Ibid.

5. Ibid., p. 16.

6. *My Angel Daniel*, above cited, p. XXI.

7. Ibid.

8. Ibid.

9. Ibid., p. XXIII.

10. Ibid., p. 81.

11. Ibid., p. 138.

12. Ibid., p. 139.

13. Ibid., p. 140-141, 143, 144-145, 145-146.

Chapter 16. OUR LADY OF EMMITSBURG

1. *Our Lady of Emmitsburg*, above cited, p. 114.

2. Ibid., p. 103.

3. Ibid., p. 107.

4. Ibid., p. 152.

5. *I am your JESUS of MERCY*, above cited, vol. 5, p. 26.

6. Ibid., vol. 2, p. 10.

7. Ibid., vol. 1, p. 135.

8. Ibid., vol. 5, p. 3.

9. Ibid., p. 41.

10. Ibid., p. 53.

11. Ibid., vol. 2, p. 32.

12. Ibid., p. 33.

13. Ibid., p. 28.

14. Ibid., vol. 5, p. 37.

15. *Our Lady of Emmitsburg*, above cited, p. 141.

16. *I am your JESUS of MERCY*, above cited, vol. 1, p. 12.

17. Ibid., p. 15.

18. Ibid., p. 19.
19. Ibid., vol. 6, p. 24.
20. *Way of Perfection*, above cited, vol. 2, p. 128.
21. Ibid., p. 134.

Chapter 17 SECOND COMING

1. *Vassula of the Sacred Heart's Passion* by Michael O'Carroll C.S.S.p., published by J.M.J. Publications, PO Box 385, Belfast BT9 6RQ, Northern Ireland, 1993, p. 55.
2. Ibid.
3. Ibid., p. 57.
4. Ibid.
5. Ibid., p. 58.
6. Ibid., p. 65.
7. Ibid., p. 139.
8. Ibid., p. 141.
9. Ibid.
10. Ibid., p. 143.
11. *Vassula Enigma*, above cited, p. 20.
12. *I am your JESUS of MERCY*, above cited, vol.1, p. 134.
13. INTRODUCTION to *My Dear Ones...MERCY*, published by the Queenship Publishing CO., above cited, 1994.
14. *Our Lady of Emmitsburg*, above cited, p.148.
15. *Spark from Heaven*, above cited, p. 21.